Saint Bernadette of Lourdes

Saint Bernadette of Lourdes

The Girl Who Saw Mary

Written and Illustrated by

Ahn Jin-a

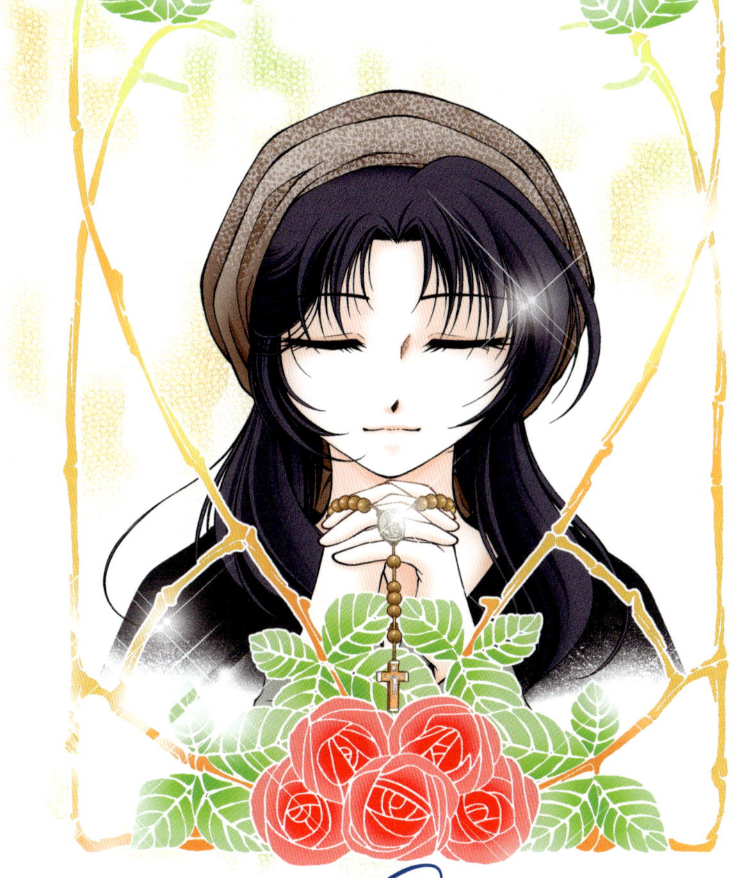

Library of Congress Control Number: 2020933508
CIP data is available.

ISBN 10: 0–8198–9101–0
ISBN 13: 978–0-8198–9101–3

루르드의 베르나데트 (Bernadette the Virgin of Lourdes) by AHN Jin-a

Originally published by Pauline Books & Media, Seoul, Korea.

Translated by Unsung Hwang

Published by Pauline Books & Media, 50 Saint Paul's Avenue,
Boston, MA 02130–3491

Printed in the U.S.A.

SBOL VSAUSAPEOILL6-1010210 9101-0

www.pauline.org

Pauline Books & Media is the publishing house of the Daughters of St. Paul, an international congregation of women religious serving the Church with the communications media.

2 3 4 5 6 7 8 9 29 28 27 26 25 24

CONTENTS

A Poor and Unfortunate Girl

MY SWEET BABY,
BERNADETTE.
방긋
HEE HEE

BERNADETTE!
DADDY!
GRIND
쿠르릉
SOUBIROUS, CAN YOU PLEASE GRIND MY GRAIN FOR CREDIT? I'LL PAY YOU BACK.
GRIND
쿠르릉
SOUBIROUS, BECAUSE OF THIS YEAR'S FAMINE, I DON'T HAVE ANY GRAIN TO GRIND AT YOUR MILL.
I'M ENDING OUR CONTRACT.
쿠릉...
GRIND
I CAN'T PAY YOU BACK NOW. I'LL HAVE THE MONEY LATER.
삐걱!
SCREECH
...
끼익...
SCREECH

1854

SOUBIROUS, DO YOU KNOW HOW MANY MONTHS OF RENT YOU'VE MISSED?

I WON'T PUT UP WITH THIS ANYMORE! GET OUT!

콜록 콜록

COUGH COUGH

THIS OLD JAIL HAS BEEN ABANDONED BECAUSE NOT EVEN PRISONERS COULD LIVE HERE.
BUT WE CAN'T AFFORD ANY OTHER PLACE.
끼익
CREAK . . .

SCAMPER!
사사삭
WHEW! THIS PLACE . . .
I GUESS IT'S BETTER THAN NOTHING.
냄새
SMELLY
웩!
BLECH!
안절
OH NO!
BERNADETTE!
부절
BERNADETTE! WHAT'S WRONG? ARE YOU OKAY?
COUGH COUGH
쿨럭쿨럭

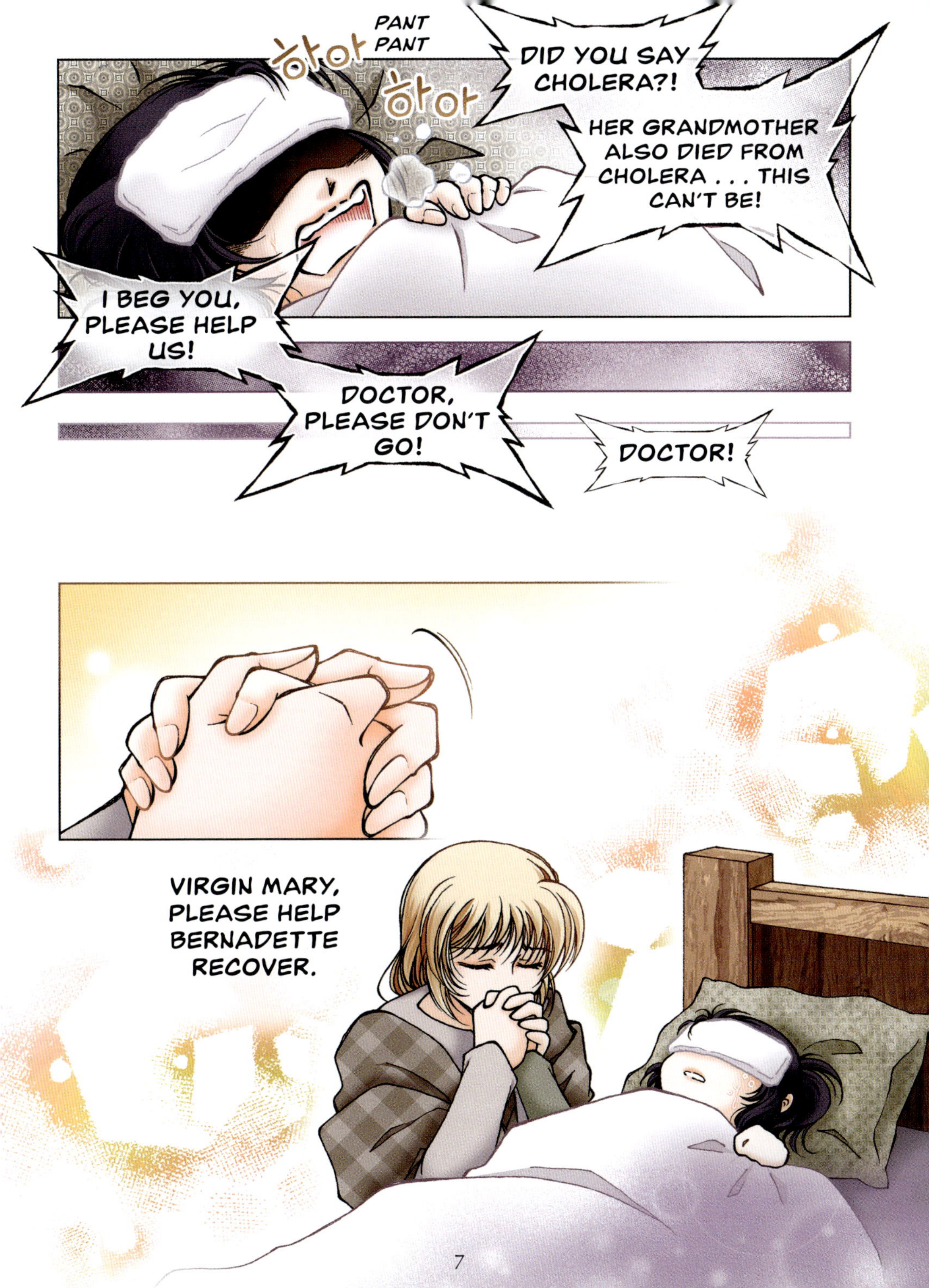
하아 하아
PANT PANT
DID YOU SAY CHOLERA?!
HER GRANDMOTHER ALSO DIED FROM CHOLERA . . . THIS CAN'T BE!
I BEG YOU, PLEASE HELP US!
DOCTOR, PLEASE DON'T GO!
DOCTOR!
VIRGIN MARY, PLEASE HELP BERNADETTE RECOVER.

달그락
CLACK
OH NO, CORN SOUP AGAIN?
IT ISN'T GOOD TO COMPLAIN ABOUT FOOD. WE SHOULD THANK GOD FOR WHAT WE DO HAVE.
AMEN.
아멘 –
THEN WHY DO YOU ONLY GIVE BREAD TO BERNADETTE?
BERNADETTE HAS POOR HEALTH.

IT'S NOT FAIR!
GIVE ME BREAD TOO! I WANT BREAD!
MY GOODNESS . . . THIS CHILD . . .
. . .
골록
COUGH COUGH
골록
골록
COUGH COUGH
골록
골록
COUGH
I'M WORRIED ABOUT BERNADETTE. HER ASTHMA SEEMS TO BE GETTING WORSE.
쌔액 쌔액
WHEEZE WHEEZE

WHAT SHOULD WE DO . . . ?
HER HEALTH WILL ONLY DECLINE IN THIS KIND OF ENVIRONMENT . . .
IT'S HARD TO GET BREAD, LET ALONE CORN TO FEED OUR CHILDREN.
I WILL TRY TO FIND MORE WORK . . . BUT GOD WILL PROVIDE.
MARCH 27, 1857
SLAM!

OFFICER, THAT'S HIM! HE STOLE FLOUR FROM MY HOUSE!
Flour
WHAT?! THAT'S NOT TRUE! WHY WOULD I STEAL OTHER PEOPLE'S THINGS?
QUIET! YOU THIEVING BEGGARS ARE ALL THE SAME!
NO, OFFICER! MY HUSBAND WOULD NEVER DO SOMETHING LIKE THAT!
!!!

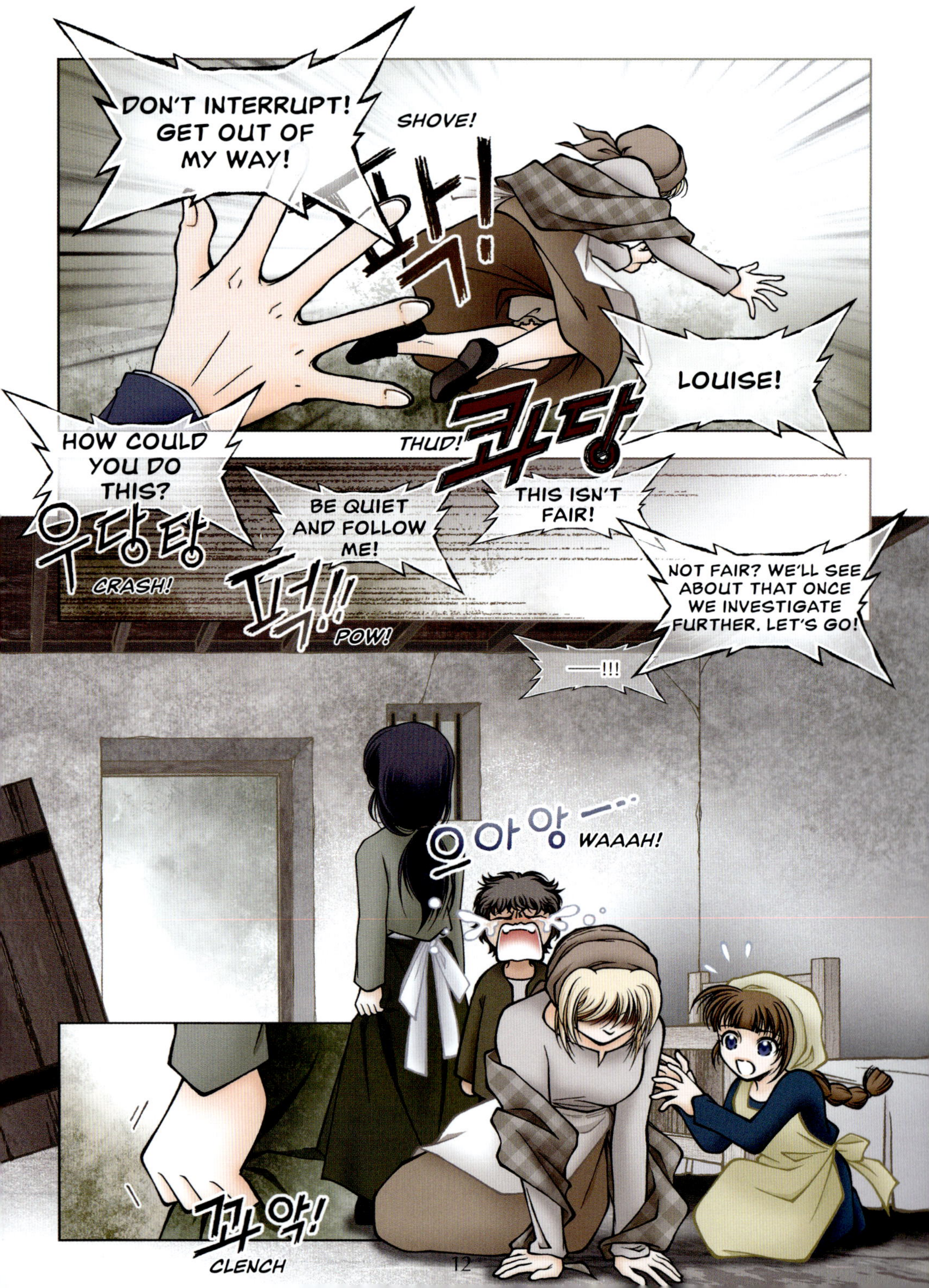
DON'T INTERRUPT! GET OUT OF MY WAY!
SHOVE!
확!
LOUISE!
콰당
THUD!
HOW COULD YOU DO THIS?
우당탕
CRASH!
BE QUIET AND FOLLOW ME!
퍽!!
POW!
THIS ISN'T FAIR!
NOT FAIR? WE'LL SEE ABOUT THAT ONCE WE INVESTIGATE FURTHER. LET'S GO!
—!!!
으아앙—
WAAAH!
꽈악!
CLENCH

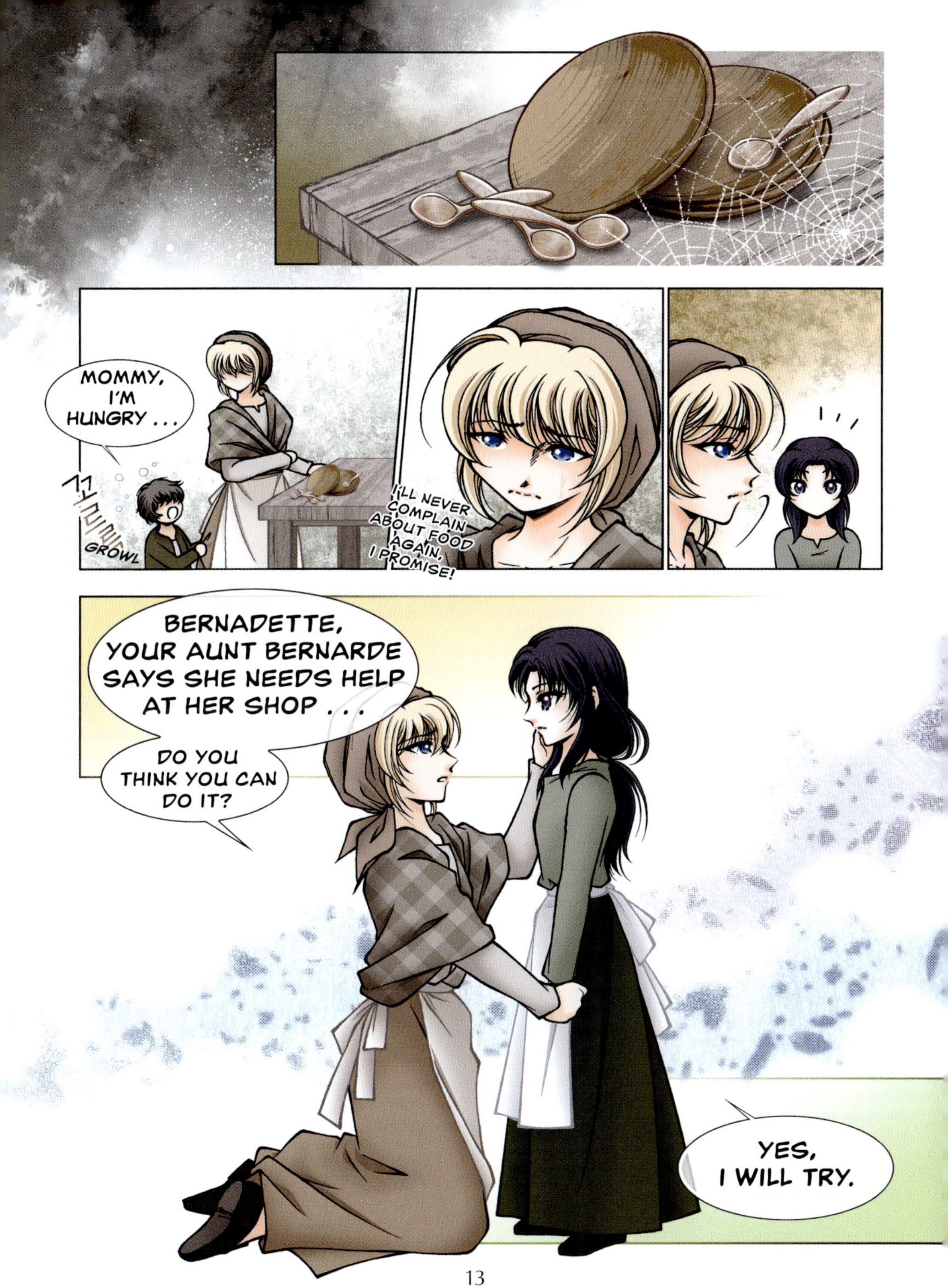

BERNADETTE, YOUR AUNT BERNARDE SAYS SHE NEEDS HELP AT HER SHOP . . .

DO YOU THINK YOU CAN DO IT?

YES, I WILL TRY.

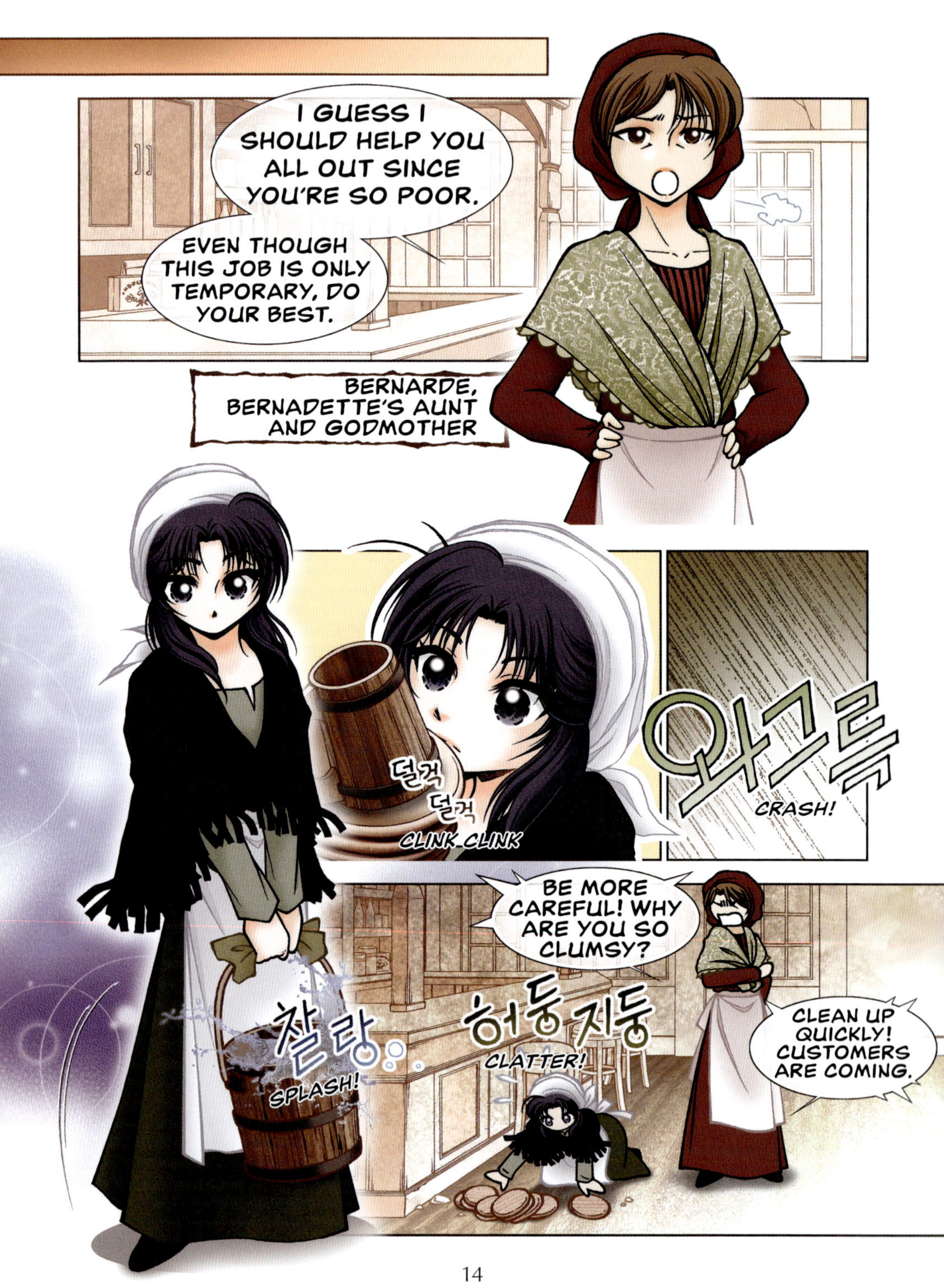
I GUESS I SHOULD HELP YOU ALL OUT SINCE YOU'RE SO POOR.
EVEN THOUGH THIS JOB IS ONLY TEMPORARY, DO YOUR BEST.
BERNARDE, BERNADETTE'S AUNT AND GODMOTHER
덜걱 덜걱
CLINK CLINK
와그르
CRASH!
찰랑
SPLASH!
허둥지둥
CLATTER!
BE MORE CAREFUL! WHY ARE YOU SO CLUMSY?
CLEAN UP QUICKLY! CUSTOMERS ARE COMING.

FULL PLATE
푸짐
WOW! THAT'S A LOT! THANKS!
BERNADETTE, DIDN'T I TELL YOU NOT TO GIVE THE CUSTOMERS SO MUCH FOOD?
BERNADETTE . . .
IT'S NOT MUCH, BUT HERE IS YOUR PAY.
I ALSO PACKED SOME LEFTOVERS.
꼬옥
GRIP

I'M HOME.

DAD . . . YOU'RE BACK?
BERNADETTE, I HEARD THAT YOU WORKED FOR YOUR AUNT WHILE I WAS GONE.

WELL DONE!
I'M PROUD OF YOU, BERNADETTE.
SINCE DAD IS HOME AND SO IS BERNADETTE, LET'S HAVE DINNER TOGETHER!
와~ 빵이다~♫
YAY! BREAD!

SHE SAYS SHE WILL TAKE YOU INTO HER HOME IF YOU TEND HER SHEEP . . .

I THINK IT WOULD BE GOOD FOR YOU TO LIVE THERE WITH HER. IT WILL ONLY BE FOR A LITTLE WHILE . . .

I'M SORRY, BERNADETTE . . .

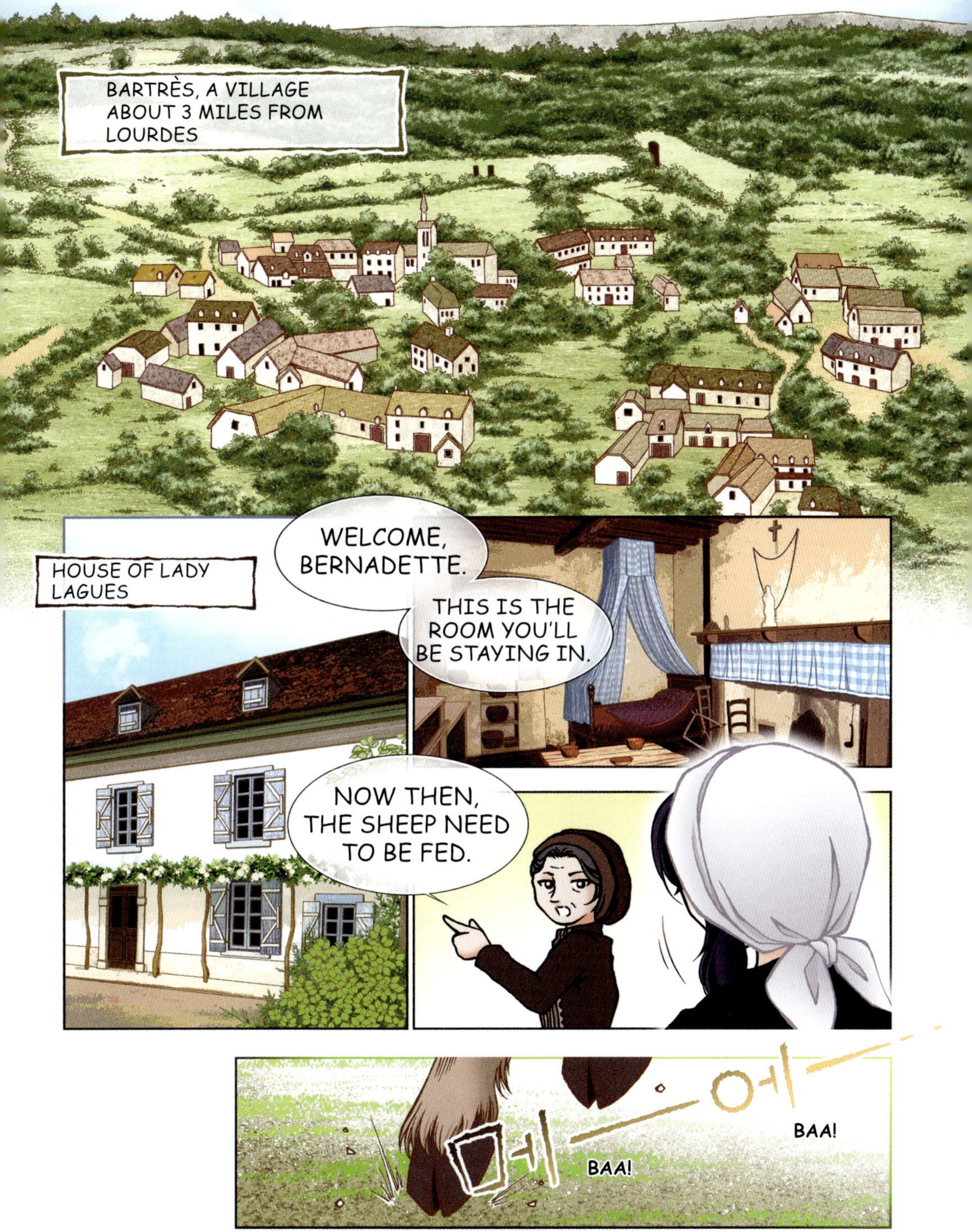

BARTRÈS, A VILLAGE ABOUT 3 MILES FROM LOURDES

HOUSE OF LADY LAGUES

WELCOME, BERNADETTE.

THIS IS THE ROOM YOU'LL BE STAYING IN.

NOW THEN, THE SHEEP NEED TO BE FED.

메-

AH, GOOD SHEEP!
쓰담 쓰담
NUDGE

SISTER, TAKE MY ROSARY WHEN YOU GO TO BARTRÈS. IT WILL HELP YOU WHILE YOU'RE AWAY FROM HOME.
WHAT? YOU WANT TO ATTEND SCHOOL?

THIS IS TERRIBLE . . .

I WON'T HAVE ANYONE TO CARE FOR MY SHEEP IF SHE GOES TO SCHOOL . . .

BERNADETTE, READ OUT LOUD FROM THE TOP OF PAGE ONE.
SPEAK UP NICE AND CLEAR.
WHAT'S WRONG? WHY AREN'T YOU READING?
UMM . . . I . . . UMM . . .

팍!
SMACK!
!!!
CRASH!
콰당탕!!
YOU'RE TESTING MY PATIENCE!
HOW CAN YOU CAN BE SO DUMB?
IF I HADN'T LOST MY OWN SON I NEVER WOULD
HAVE NURSED YOU OR TRIED TO TEACH YOU.

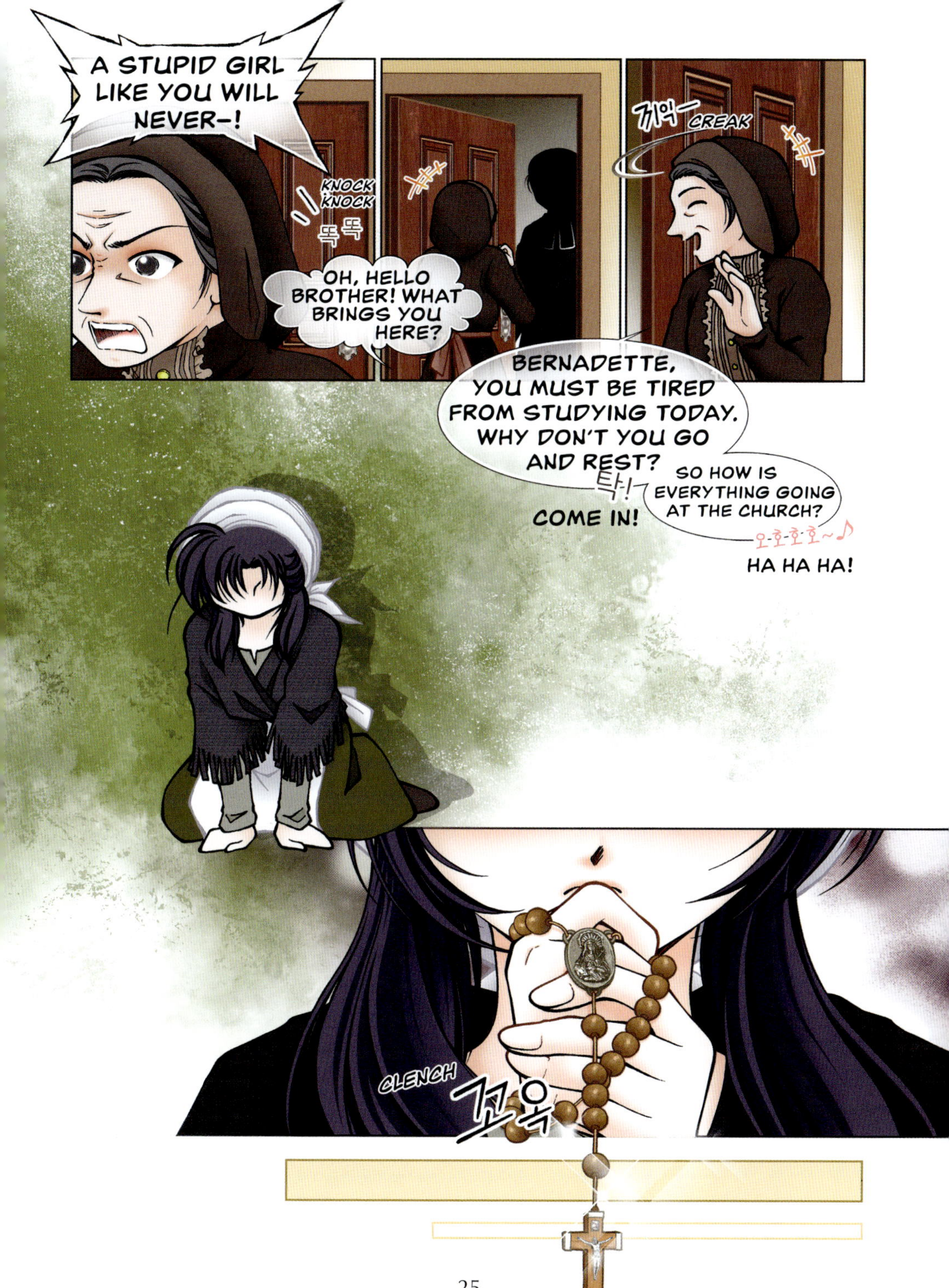
A STUPID GIRL LIKE YOU WILL NEVER-!
KNOCK KNOCK
똑똑
OH, HELLO BROTHER! WHAT BRINGS YOU HERE?
끼익- CREAK
BERNADETTE, YOU MUST BE TIRED FROM STUDYING TODAY. WHY DON'T YOU GO AND REST?
탁!
COME IN!
SO HOW IS EVERYTHING GOING AT THE CHURCH?
오호호호~♪
HA HA HA!
CLENCH
꼬옥

JANUARY 17, 1858
TODAY IS THE DAY YOU ARE GOING TO LOURDES TO SEE YOUR FAMILY, RIGHT?

MAKE SURE YOU'LL BE BACK IN TIME TO TAKE CARE OF MY SHEEP.

. . .
. . .

ALWAYS SO QUIET! DON'T SAY ANYTHING, THEN. JUST GO.

CHURCH OF LOURDES

JANUARY 20, 1858
WHAT DID YOU SAY? TELL ME AGAIN!

THE PRIEST TOLD ME THAT
I NEED TO RECEIVE MY FIRST HOLY COMMUNION.
SO I MUST RETURN TO LOURDES.
...
FINE.
IF THE PRIEST SAYS SO, I CAN'T SAY NO. YOU MAY GO.

GRIP
꼬옥
WHAT'S THAT?
멈칫

A Lady from Heaven

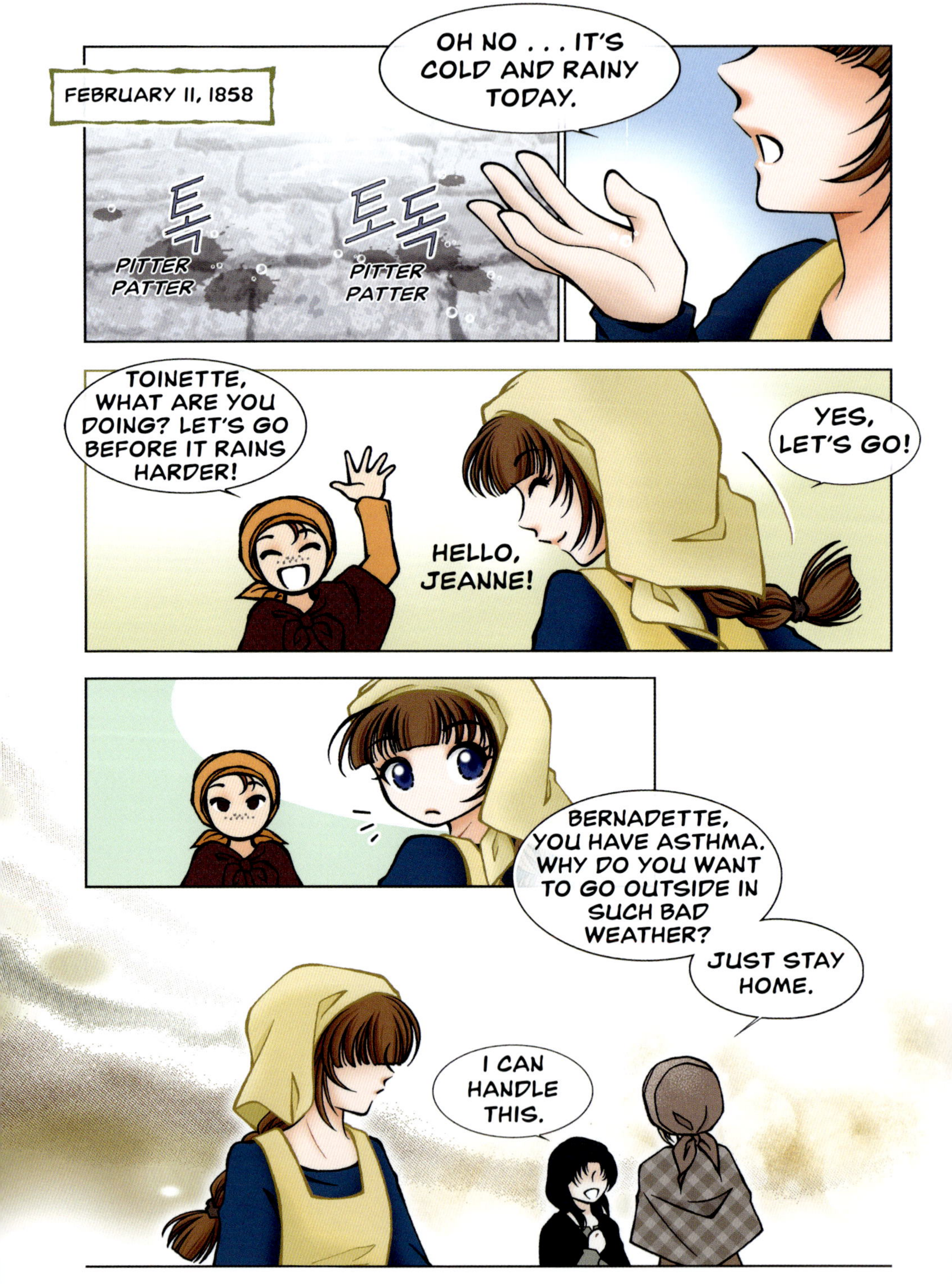

BERNADETTE, YOU HAVE ASTHMA. WHY DO YOU WANT TO GO OUTSIDE IN SUCH BAD WEATHER?

JUST STAY HOME.

I CAN HANDLE THIS.

SWISH
스륵
YOU MUSTN'T CATCH A COLD.
WEAR THIS SCARF TIGHTLY OVER YOUR HEAD.
DON'T STAY OUT TOO LONG. COME BACK BEFORE SUNSET!

THEN MR. SO AND SO SAID . . .
WOW, REALLY?
THE PONT-VIEUX BRIDGE
WHERE CAN WE GATHER FIREWOOD TODAY? IT SEEMS LIKE NO MATTER WHERE WE GO, SOMEONE GETS MAD AT US FOR TAKING IT.
IT WOULD BE GOOD IF IT'S SOMEPLACE NEARBY . . .
I HATE IT WHEN THE GROWNUPS ACT LIKE WE'RE TAKING THEIR WOOD. THEY TREAT US LIKE THIEVES.
WAIT, I KNOW! LET'S GO BY THE GAVE RIVER.
GOOD IDEA! NO ONE WILL BOTHER US THERE.

GROTTO OF MASSABIELLE
YIKES, IT'S COLD!
참방
SPLASH
SPLISH SPLASH
참방
참방
SPLASH
참방
LET'S CROSS QUICKLY!
AH, MY FEET ARE COLD!
안절부절
UMM . . .
WOW, THERE ARE SO MANY BRANCHES!
EVEN THOUGH MY FEET ARE COLD, I'M GLAD WE CAME HERE.
머뭇머뭇
SHIVER SHIVER

HEY! COULD YOU PLEASE THROW SOME ROCKS IN THE STREAM FOR ME TO STEP ON SO I CAN CROSS TOO?

WHY ARE YOU CAUSING EXTRA WORK FOR US? JUST CROSS THE STREAM!

WHY DID SHE COME ALONG AT ALL? WHAT A PAIN.

I DON'T KNOW.

IF YOU DON'T WANT TO, JUST GO HOME!

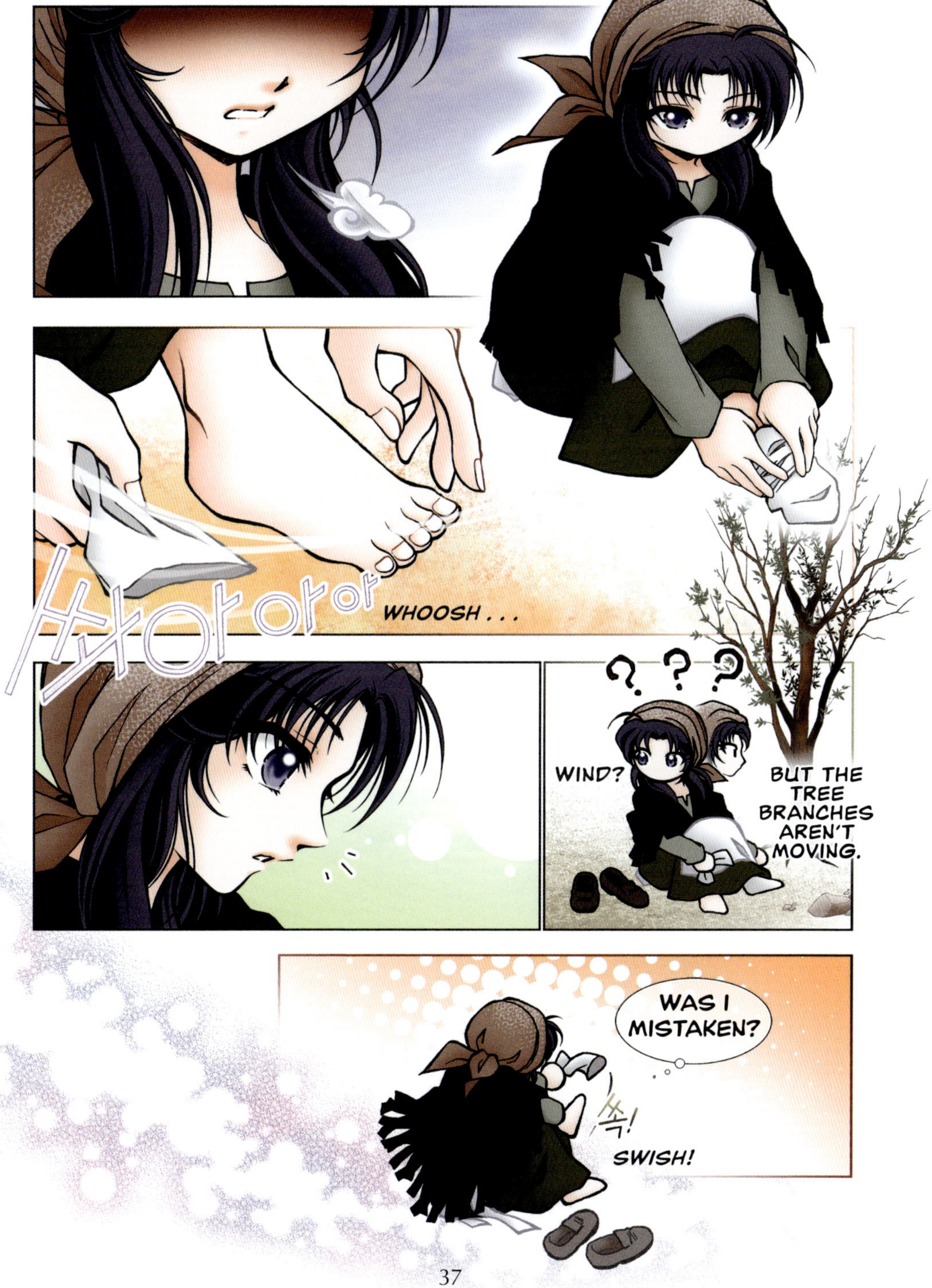

쏴아아아아

WHOOSH . . .

WIND?

BUT THE TREE BRANCHES AREN'T MOVING.

WHOOSH . . .

살랑
살랑
RUSTLE
RUSTLE

바들
TREMBLE
TREMBLE
바들

SHE DISAPPEARED.
WHO WAS THAT?
참방
SPLASH
SHE WAS SO BEAUTIFUL AND MYSTERIOUS . . .
THE WATER ISN'T COLD!

BRRR . . . I'M SO COLD. SINCE WE GATHERED ENOUGH FIREWOOD . . .
LET'S HEAD HOME BEFORE IT GETS DARK.

WE'RE FREEZING . . .
BUT MY WEAK SISTER DOESN'T LOOK COLD AT ALL.

SHE EVEN HAS MORE BRANCHES THAN I DO!

HOW DID YOU CROSS THE COLD STREAM?

HUH? IT WASN'T COLD.

WEREN'T YOU JUST TEASING ME BY PRETENDING IT WAS COLD?

BRRR . . .
덜덜덜

NO! IT REALLY WAS!

LOOK AT US! WE'RE STILL SHIVERING!

WHAT'S GOING ON?

TELL ME WHAT HAPPENED!

. . . CAN YOU KEEP A SECRET?
SURE! LET ME HEAR IT!
WELL . . . I MET THIS LADY AT THE GROTTO . . .

I PRAYED THE ROSARY WITH HER. SHE WAS WRAPPED IN DAZZLING LIGHT.
THEN THE RIVER WASN'T COLD AND I WAS ABLE TO GATHER A LOT OF FIREWOOD.
. . .
덜컹
CREAK
IT'S WAY PAST SUNSET . . . COME BACK EARLIER NEXT TIME.

MOM! MOM! LISTEN TO THIS!
DO YOU KNOW WHAT BERNADETTE TOLD ME?
SHE SAID SHE SAW A LADY AT THE GROTTO OF MASSABIELLE.
SHE WAS WRAPPED IN DAZZLING LIGHT . . .
흠칫!
GASP!
WHAT ARE YOU GIRLS TAKING ABOUT? YOU'LL GET INTO TROUBLE!
YOU SHOULDN'T SHARE THIS STORY ANYWHERE!
STAY AWAY FROM THAT GROTTO!
AND STOP MAKING UP STORIES!
. . . I'M SORRY, MOM . . .

FEBRUARY 14, 1858
PSST . . .
PSST . . .
BERNADETTE, YOU'RE NOT SICK TODAY! YOU'VE BEEN MISSING A LOT OF SCHOOL . . .
BERNADETTE!
BERNADETTE, IS IT TRUE?
우르르르
CROWD

SNICKER
키득
SNICKER
키득
킥킥
SNICKER
I HEARD YOU SAW A STRANGE PERSON AT THE GROTTO.
SHE'S NOT A STRANGE PERSON! DON'T TALK LIKE THAT!
REALLY?
THEN TAKE THIS HOLY WATER AND SPRINKLE IT ON HER. PROVE IT.
IF SHE'S NOT A DEVIL IT WON'T DO ANY HARM, RIGHT?
HEY, LET'S GO TOGETHER!
SINCE WHEN ARE THEY SUCH GOOD FRIENDS WITH BERNADETTE? I'M THE ONE WHO WAS AT THE GROTTO WITH HER . . .

SEE? SHE'S OVER THERE!
. . . DO YOU SEE ANYTHING?
I'M OUT OF BREATH. WHY IS SHE SO FAST?
NO, NOTHING.
흐—헉
PANT PANT
BERNADETTE, SPRINKLE THAT HOLY WATER WE GAVE YOU.

POP!
퐁
IF YOU ARE SENT FROM GOD, PLEASE STAY . . .
. . . AND IF NOT, PLEASE GO AWAY.
촤악!
SPLASH!
SPRINKLE ALL THE HOLY WATER IN THE BOTTLE.
WE'LL HELP YOU.

HEY, LET'S JOIN IN.
촥
SPRINKLE
PSST . . .
킥킥킥♪
SNICKER
GO AWAY, DEVIL!
촤악!
SPLASH
YOU EVIL SPIRIT,
LEAVE BERNADETTE ALONE!
촥
SPLASH
GO AWAY, DEVIL!
HOW DARE THEY COME HERE WITHOUT ME!

I'LL SHOW THEM . . .

휙-!!
THUD!
TAKE THIS!

쿵!!
CRASH!!
후두둑-!
RUMBLE!
HUH? WHAT'S THAT?

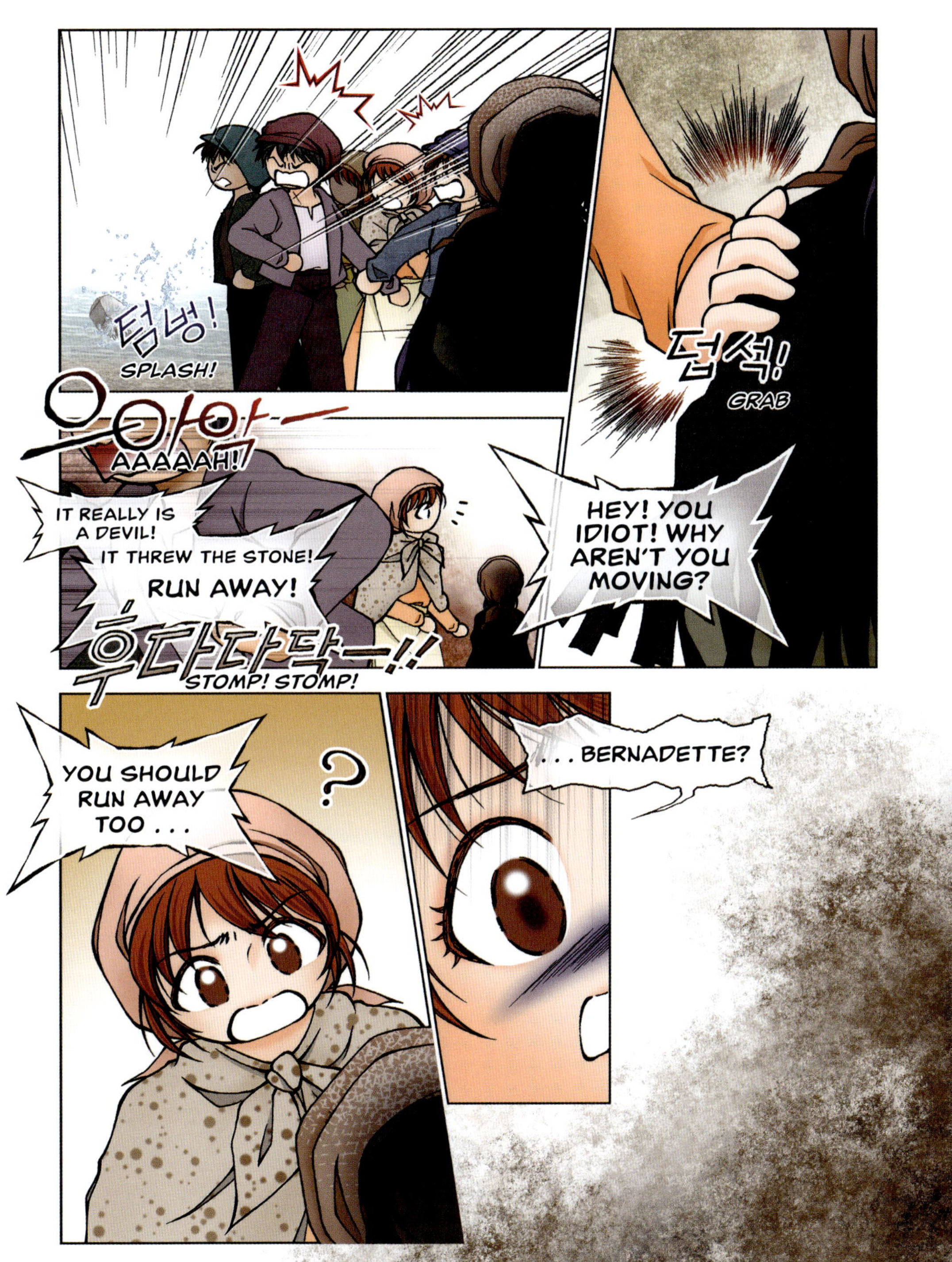

텀벙!
SPLASH!
덥석!
GRAB
우와악
AAAAAH!!
IT REALLY IS A DEVIL!
IT THREW THE STONE!
RUN AWAY!
후다다닥—!!
STOMP! STOMP!
HEY! YOU IDIOT! WHY AREN'T YOU MOVING?
YOU SHOULD RUN AWAY TOO . . .
?
. . . BERNADETTE?

MISTER, OVER THERE . . .
SHE'S THERE!

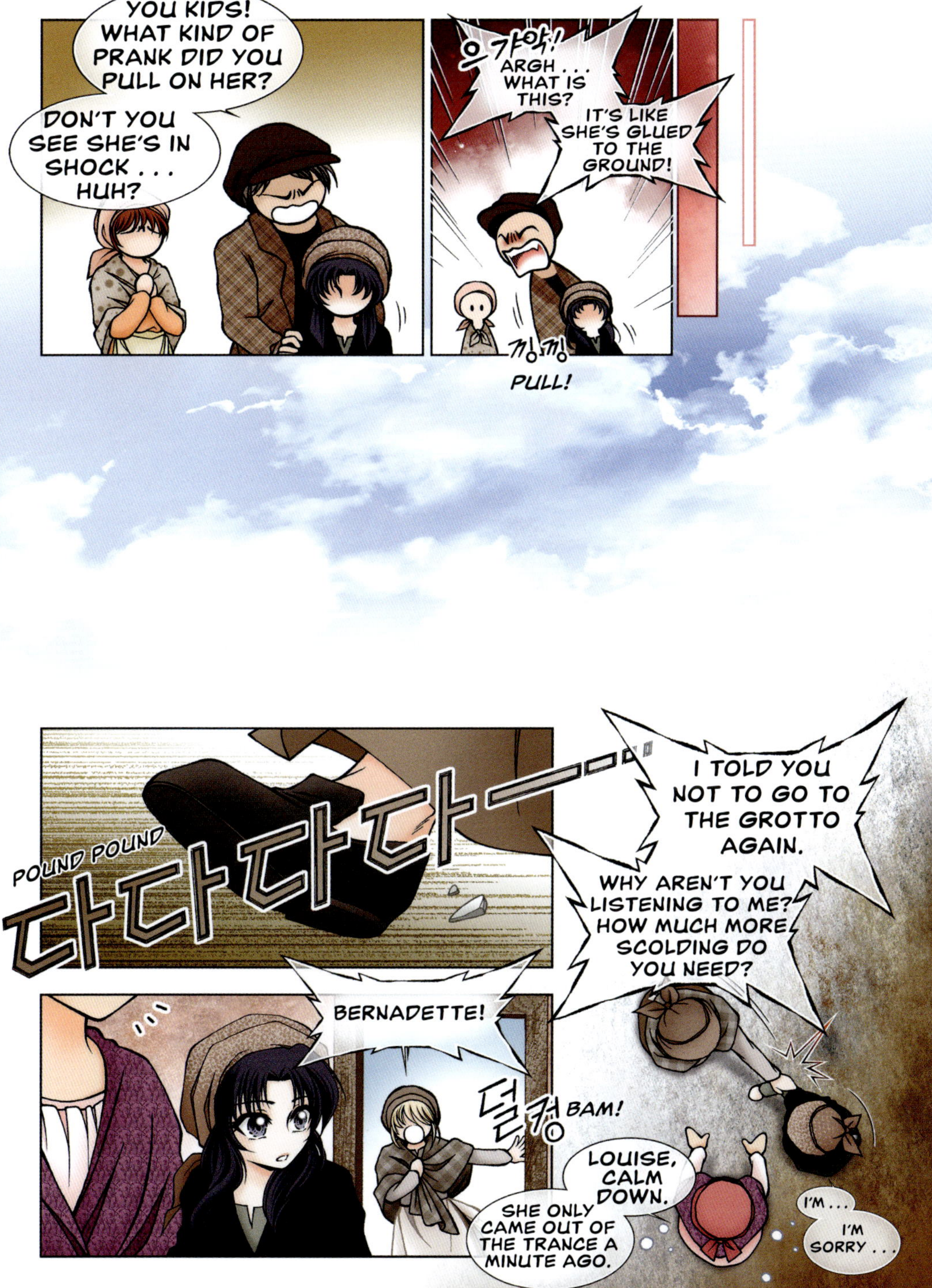

POUND POUND

다다다다—

I TOLD YOU NOT TO GO TO THE GROTTO AGAIN.

WHY AREN'T YOU LISTENING TO ME? HOW MUCH MORE SCOLDING DO YOU NEED?

BERNADETTE!

...

덜컹

BAM!

LOUISE, CALM DOWN.

SHE ONLY CAME OUT OF THE TRANCE A MINUTE AGO.

I'M . . . I'M SORRY . . .

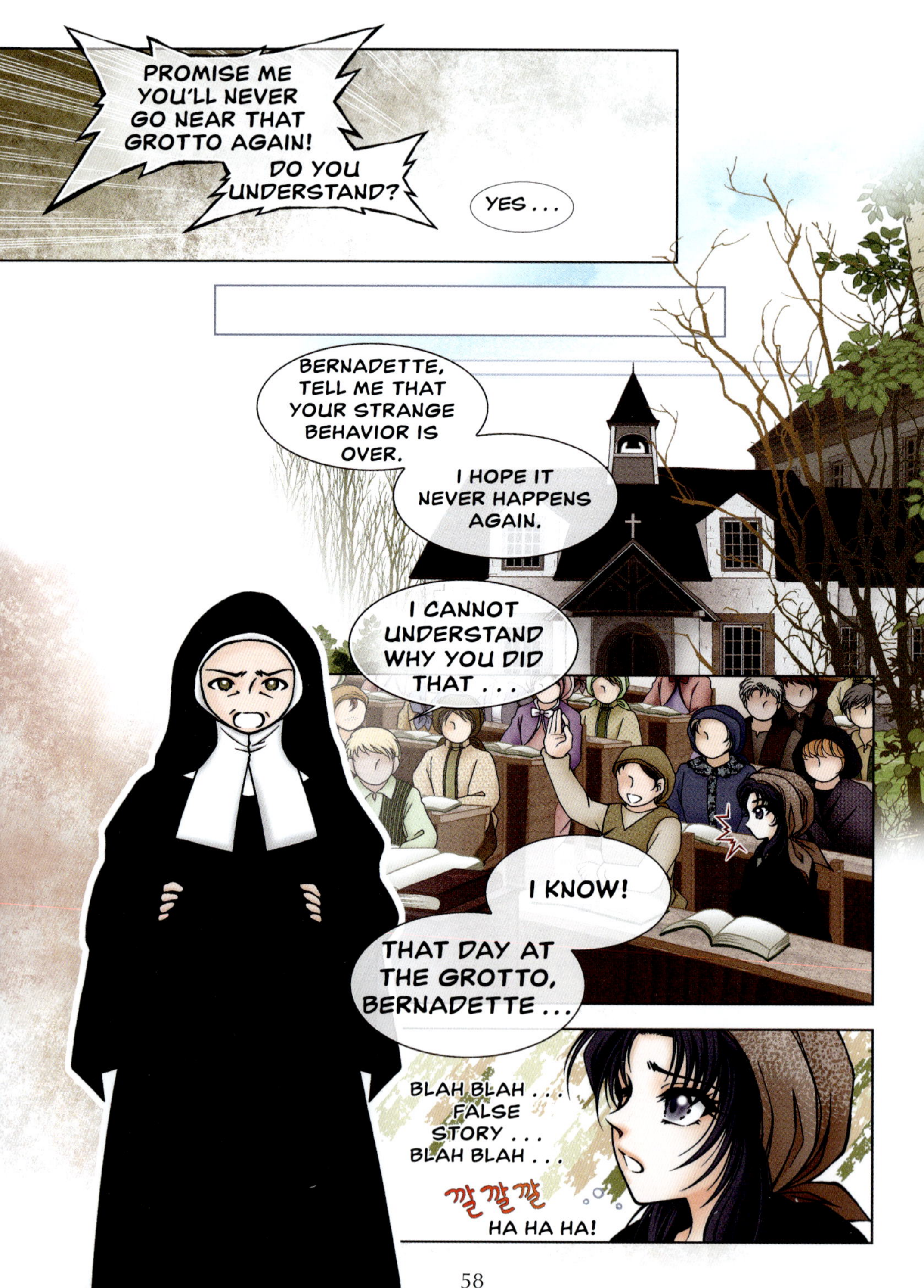
PROMISE ME YOU'LL NEVER GO NEAR THAT GROTTO AGAIN!
DO YOU UNDERSTAND?
YES . . .
BERNADETTE, TELL ME THAT YOUR STRANGE BEHAVIOR IS OVER.
I HOPE IT NEVER HAPPENS AGAIN.
I CANNOT UNDERSTAND WHY YOU DID THAT . . .
I KNOW!
THAT DAY AT THE GROTTO, BERNADETTE . . .
BLAH BLAH . . . FALSE STORY . . . BLAH BLAH . . .
깔깔깔
HA HA HA!

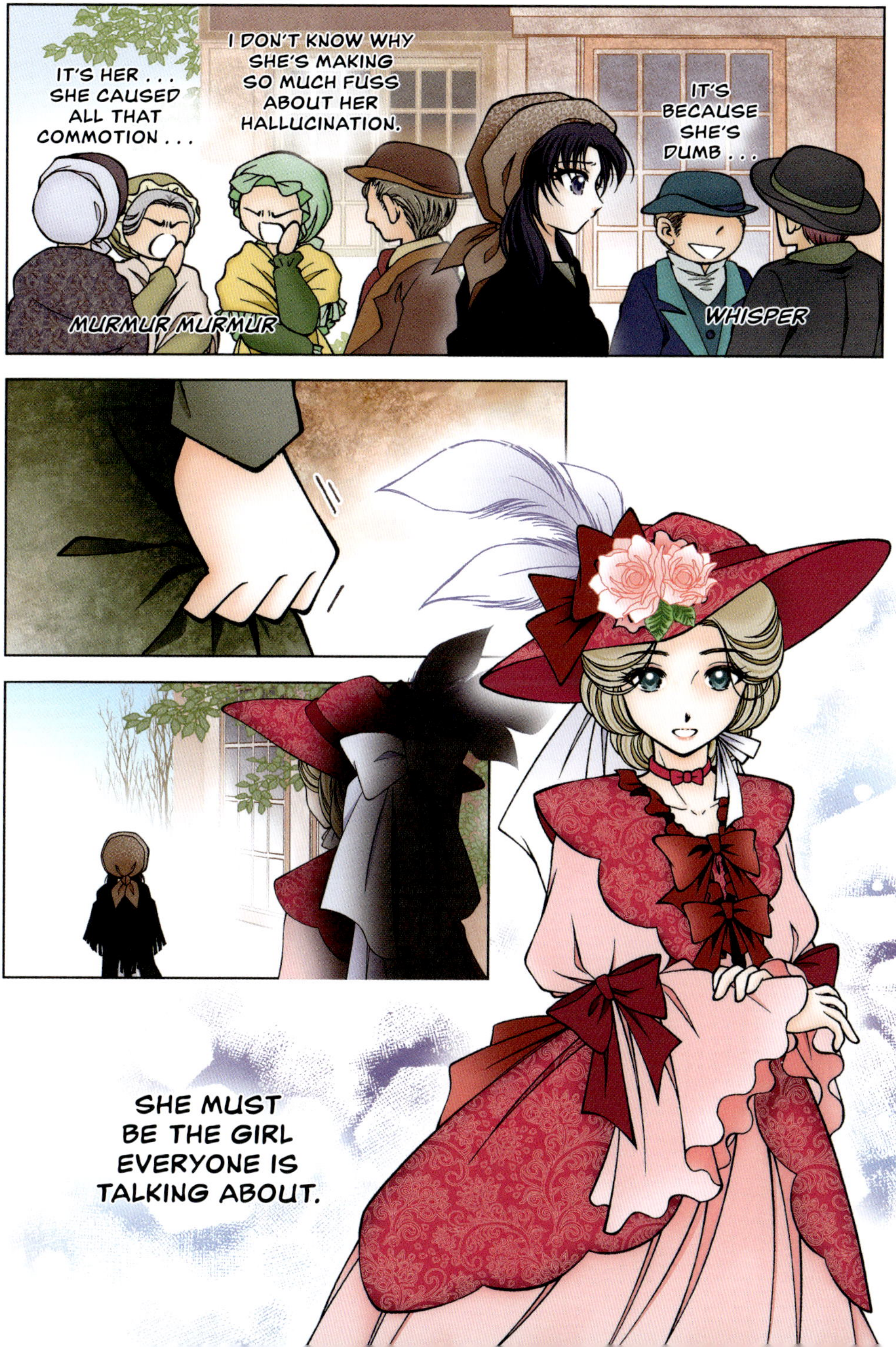

SHE MUST BE THE GIRL EVERYONE IS TALKING ABOUT.

HERE YOU GO, MADAM MILLET, JUST AS YOU ASKED.
OH, LOUISE. THANK YOU SO MUCH.

CALL ME ANY TIME YOU HAVE SOME WORK FOR ME TO DO.
LOUISE, WAIT.

I HAVE A FAVOR TO ASK YOU.

. . . REALLY? WHAT IS IT?
I WANT YOU TO KEEP THIS BETWEEN YOU AND ME.
PLEASE.

BERNADETTE, I GIVE YOU PERMISSION TO GO TO THE GROTTO,
BUT YOU NEED TO DO SOMETHING FOR ME NEARBY.
깜짝
GASP!
FEBRUARY 18, 1858
I'M SORRY IF I STARTLED YOU, BERNADETTE.
I'D LIKE YOU TO DO SOMETHING FOR ME.
PLEASE ASK THE LADY APPEARING AT THE GROTTO TO WRITE HER NAME ON THIS PAPER.
THANK YOU.

WILL YOU PLEASE
WRITE YOU NAME
FOR ME?
THAT ISN'T
NECESSARY.

A Promise for Fifteen Days

BUT THE WORDS AND ACTIONS OF THIS CHILD SEEM GENUINE.

SHE MUST HAVE SEEN SOMETHING.

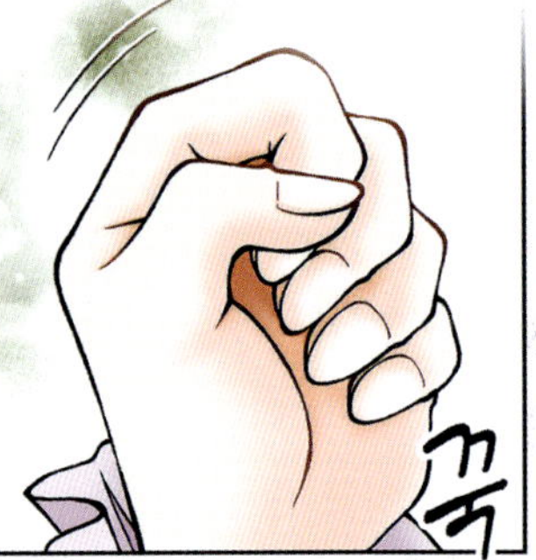

CLENCH

THAT'S IT!
I WILL TAKE HER UNDER
MY CARE FROM
NOW ON!

MURMUR MURMUR
와글 와글
TSK!
쯧!

CAUGHT YOU, YOU LITTLE BRAT!
GRAB!
덥석!
BERNADETTE!
WHY ARE YOU DOING THIS? LET HER GO!
STAY BACK! IF YOU INTERFERE, WE'LL ARREST YOU TOO.
FOLLOW ME!
ARE YOU THE GIRL WHO GOES TO THE GROTTO EVERY DAY?
YES.
NAME?
BERNADETTE.
SO YOU SAW THE VIRGIN MARY AT THE GROTTO?
I NEVER SAID SHE WAS THE VIRGIN MARY.
I SAID I SAW A LADY SURROUNDED BY DAZZLING LIGHT.
WHY DID YOU GO TO THE GROTTO?
AND HOW DID YOU SEE HER?
I WENT FOR FIREWOOD.
I LOOKED UP WHEN I HEARD THE WIND BLOWING AND SAW THE LADY THERE.
NO ONE ELSE HAS SEEN THE LADY EXCEPT YOU.
YOU ARE LYING.
NO, I REALLY DID SEE THE LADY.
I PROMISED HER I WOULD GO TO THE GROTTO FOR FIFTEEN DAYS.
YOU'RE GOING TO CONTINUE LYING?
YOUR STUPID LIE IS CAUSING A LOT OF TROUBLE!
I'M NOT LYING.

NOT LYING?!
IF YOU CONTINUE WITH THIS STORY I'LL LOCK YOU UP IN JAIL!
DO AS YOU WISH, CHIEF OFFICER!
BERNADETTE.
SOUBIROUS! ISN'T THIS ALL PART OF YOUR SCHEME?
. . . MY SCHEME?
WHAT ARE YOU TALKING ABOUT?
USING THAT DUMB DAUGHTER OF YOURS.
AREN'T YOU TRYING TO MAKE MONEY BY GETTING PEOPLE INVOLVED IN THIS RACKET?
NO, NEVER!
I TOLD MY DAUGHTER NOT TO GO TO THE GROTTO.
HA! IF THAT'S TRUE,
TAKE BETTER CARE OF DISCIPLINING HER! I WON'T BE EASY ON HER NEXT TIME!

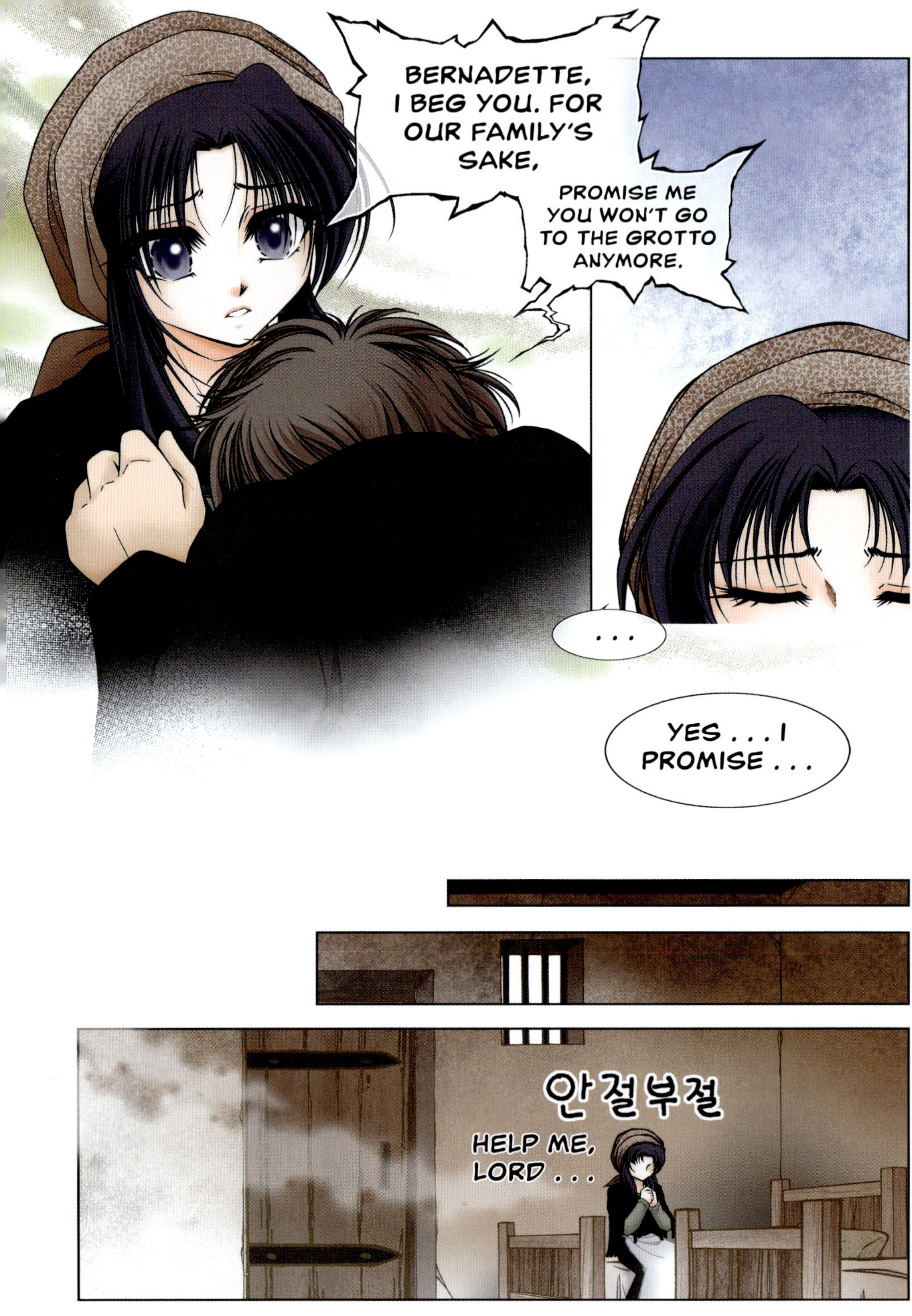

BERNADETTE, I BEG YOU. FOR OUR FAMILY'S SAKE,

PROMISE ME YOU WON'T GO TO THE GROTTO ANYMORE.

. . .

YES . . . I PROMISE . . .

GLANCE
힐끔
슥
REACH
TREMBLE
멈칫
BERNADETTE, WILL YOU DO ME THE FAVOR OF COMING HERE FOR FIFTEEN DAYS?
BERNADETTE, I BEG YOU.
FOR OUR FAMILY'S SAKE, PROMISE ME YOU WON'T GO TO THE GROTTO ANYMORE.

BERNADETTE, COME TO THIS GROTTO FOR FIFTEEN DAYS . . .

BERNADETTE, FOR OUR FAMILY'S SAKE . . .

I NEED TO KEEP MY PROMISE TO THE LADY.

BUT . . .

I MADE A PROMISE TO MOM AND DAD TOO . . .

BERNADETTE, FOR FIFTEEN DAYS . . .

BERNADETTE, YOU MUST NOT GO . . . !

BERNADETTE!

끼익
CREAK . . .
TIP-TOE
살금

IT'S LATE. YOU SHOULD BE IN BED.
OKAY.

ONCE BERNADETTE HAS SET HER MIND ON SOMETHING, NOTHING CAN STOP HER . . .
하아
SIGH.

HEY,
DID YOU HEAR THE RUMOR THAT'S BEEN GOING AROUND?
YES.
I HEARD IT TOO. AT LOURDES . . .
THERE'S A GIRL WHO SAW THE VIRGIN MARY.
MURMUR MURMUR
우글우글
FEBRUARY 25, 1858
와글
MURMUR

KISS THE GROUND AND PRAY THAT SINNERS WILL COME BACK TO GOD.
우왕좌왕
GLANCE
LOOK FOR A SPRING AND DRINK FROM IT. THEN WASH IN IT AND EAT SOME OF THE GRASS NEARBY.
부욱 북-
SCRATCH SCRATCH

우걱 우걱
CHOMP CHOMP

철벅 철벅 철벅
SCRUB SCRUB SCRUB

윽!
YUCK!

쿨럭 쿨럭
COUGH COUGH

BERNADETTE, WHAT ARE YOU DOING?!
후다다닥
FWOOM!
YOU'RE ALREADY SICKLY. WHY ARE YOU ARE DOING THIS?
OH, WHY WON'T THIS MUD COME OFF YOUR FACE?
LOOK, EVERYONE!
THERE'S A SPRING HERE!

DID YOU HEAR?

HEAR WHAT?

A NEW SPRING WAS FOUND AT THE GROTTO OF MASSABIELLE.

PEOPLE ARE SAYING THAT SINCE A SPRING CAME UP WHERE THE VIRGIN MARY APPEARED,

THE SPRING WATER MUST HAVE SPECIAL PROPERTIES.

SPECIAL PROPERTIES?

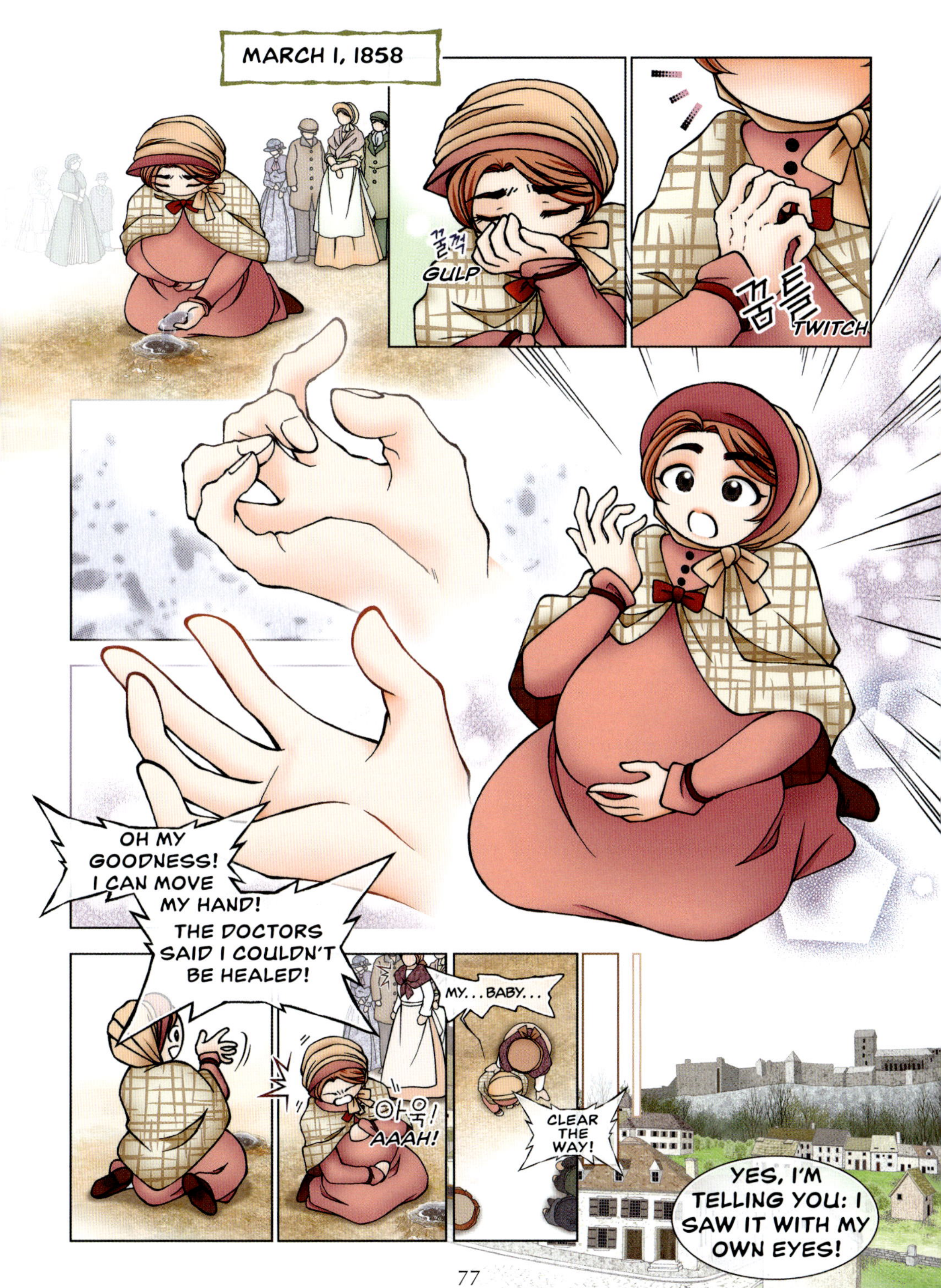
MARCH 1, 1858
꿀꺽
GULP
꿈틀
TWITCH
OH MY GOODNESS! I CAN MOVE MY HAND!
THE DOCTORS SAID I COULDN'T BE HEALED!
아욱!
AAAH!
MY... BABY...
CLEAR THE WAY!
YES, I'M TELLING YOU: I SAW IT WITH MY OWN EYES!

AFTER DRINKING WATER FROM THE SPRING, A PREGNANT LADY WITH A PARALYZED HAND STARTED TO MOVE HER FINGERS.

NOT ONLY THAT, SHE WENT INTO LABOR ON THE SPOT

AND WALKED TO THE HOSPITAL THREE MILES AWAY ALL BY HERSELF! SHE DELIVERED A HEALTHY BABY.

WOW! THAT'S AMAZING!

AND GUESS WHAT? I HEARD THAT A MAN WITH AN INJURED LEG DRANK THE SPRING WATER

AND HIS LEG WAS HEALED RIGHT AWAY.

GULP
꿀꺽

말짱
GOOD AS NEW!

APPARENTLY THE LADY TOLD BERNADETTE THREE SECRETS . . .

SOMEONE ELSE DRANK THE WATER AND . . .

THE SPRING WATER . . .

——!

THIS MUST BE

A MIRACLE!!

THUMP THUMP
우두두둑—!!
HEY, BERNADETTE,
WHAT DID THE LADY SAY THIS TIME?
MORE SECRETS? TELL US WHAT SHE SAID!
DON'T KEEP IT TO YOURSELF! TELL US!

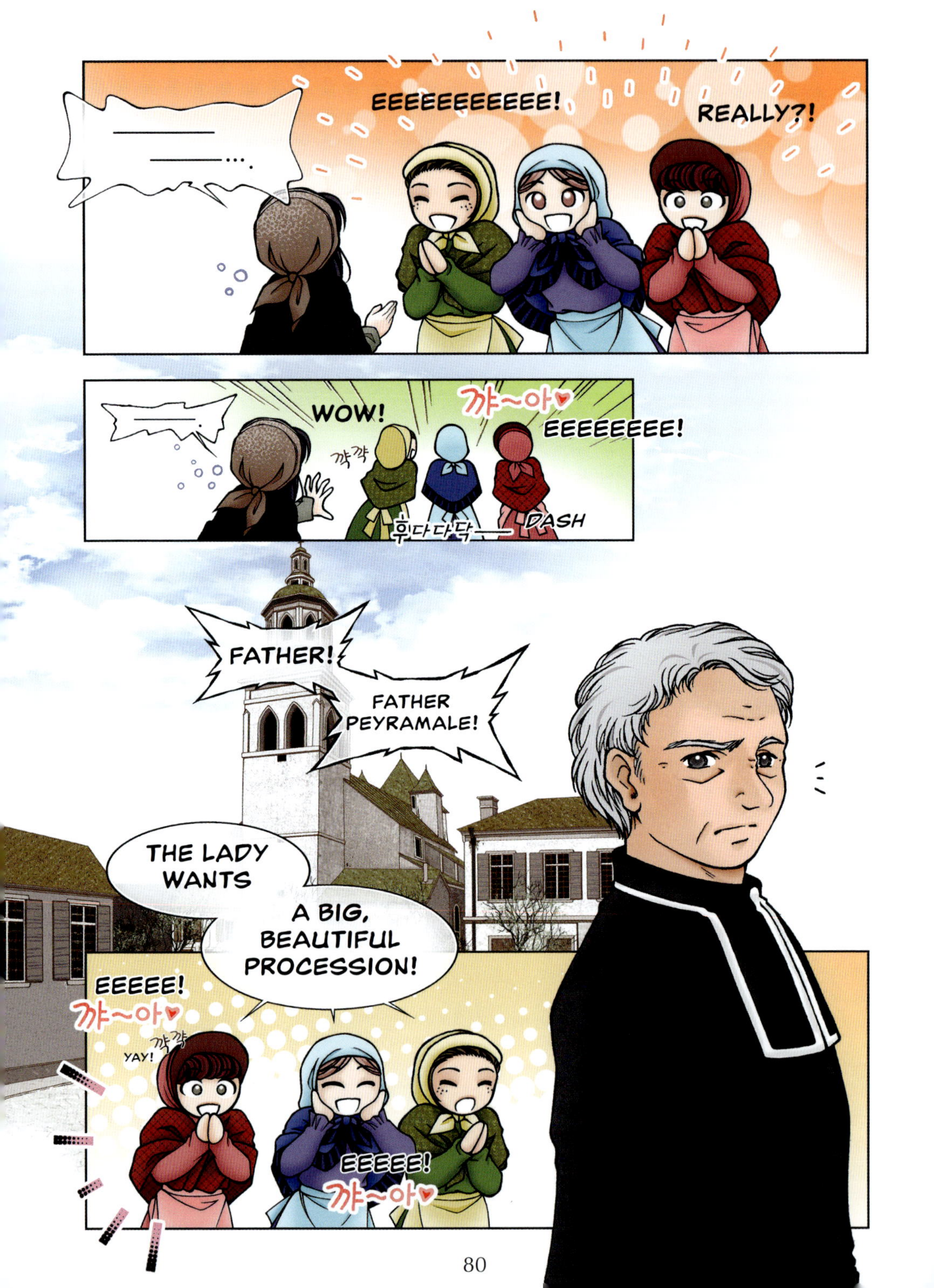

EEEEEEEEEEE!
REALLY?!

WOW!
꺄~아♥
EEEEEEEE!
꺅꺅
후다다닥
DASH
FATHER!
FATHER PEYRAMALE!
THE LADY WANTS
A BIG, BEAUTIFUL PROCESSION!
EEEEE!
꺄~아♥
꺅꺅
YAY!
EEEEEE!
꺄~아♥

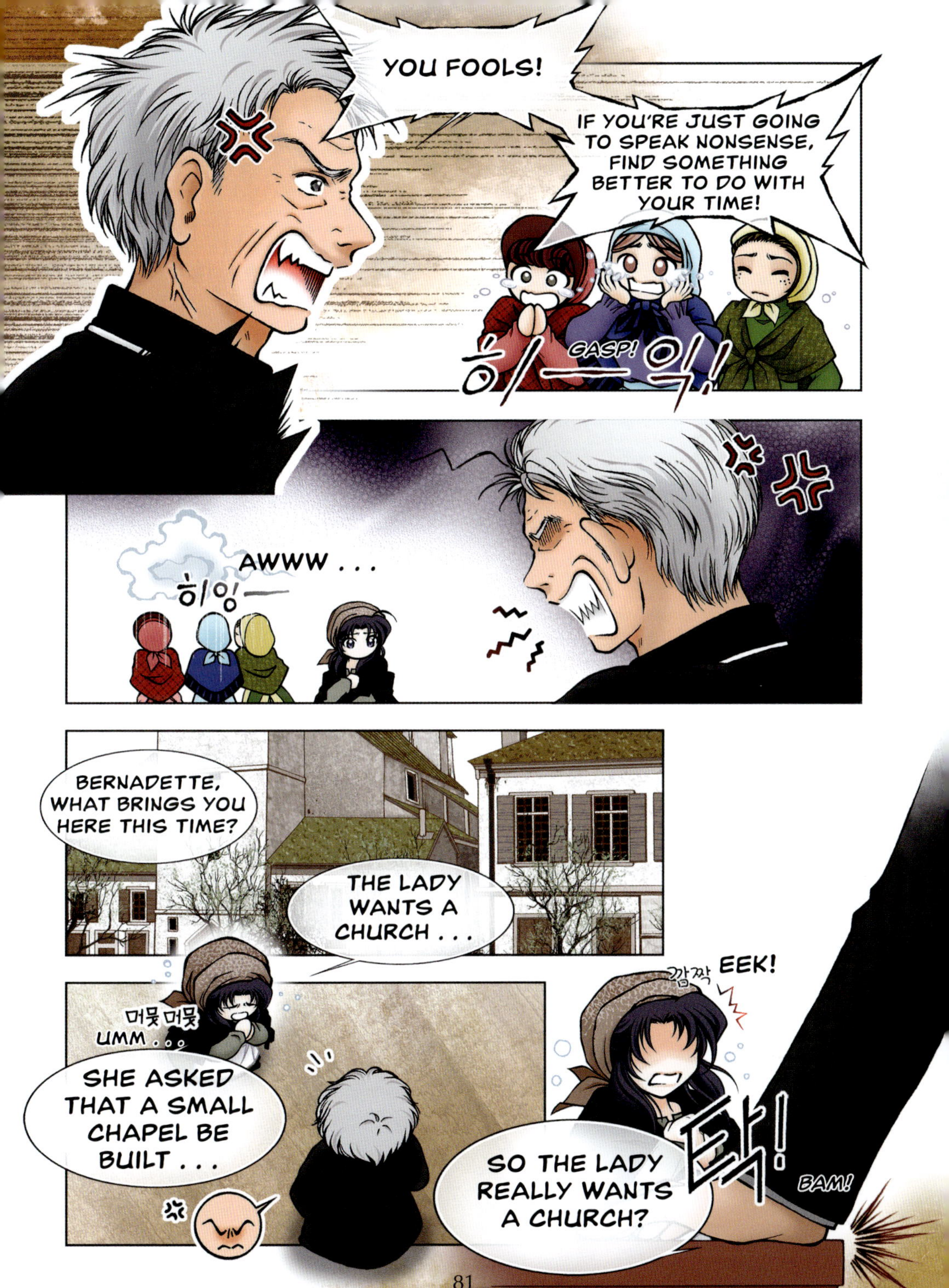

YOU FOOLS!

IF YOU'RE JUST GOING TO SPEAK NONSENSE, FIND SOMETHING BETTER TO DO WITH YOUR TIME!

히—익!

GASP!

AWWW . . .

히잉—

BERNADETTE, WHAT BRINGS YOU HERE THIS TIME?

THE LADY WANTS A CHURCH . . .

머뭇머뭇

UMM . . .

SHE ASKED THAT A SMALL CHAPEL BE BUILT . . .

깜짝

EEK!

SO THE LADY REALLY WANTS A CHURCH?

탁!

BAM!

THEN YOU MUST FIND OUT HER NAME.
ALSO, TELL HER TO MAKE ROSES BLOOM IN THE GROTTO.*
IF THAT HAPPENS, I'LL BUILD HER A BIG CHURCH, NOT A SMALL ONE!
NOW GO HOME!
*THIS WAS IN EARLY MARCH. ROSES BLOOM BETWEEN MAY AND JUNE.

MARCH 4, 1858
WOW, LOOK AT ALL THE PEOPLE WHO CAME! EVERYONE WANTS TO CATCH A GLIMPSE OF THE VIRGIN MARY!
HEY, STOP PUSHING ME!
THERE'S NO ROOM TO MOVE!
CHATTER CHATTER
와글 와글
IT'S PROBABLY BECAUSE TODAY IS THE LAST OF THE FIFTEEN DAYS BERNADETTE PROMISED TO COME TO THE GROTTO.
SOMETHING BIG HAS TO HAPPEN . . . DO YOU THINK SHE'LL TELL US THE SECRETS THE LADY REVEALED TO HER?
우글
CHATTER
WE'RE GOING TO SEE A MIRACLE TODAY!
CHATTER CHATTER
웅성 웅성

RISE

WHAT? IT ENDED?

THAT'S IT?

MURMUR

AWW . . . I THOUGHT I WAS GOING TO SEE A MIRACLE . . .

MURMUR MURMUR

NOT ONLY WAS THERE NO MIRACLE . . .

. . . NOTHING HAPPENED!

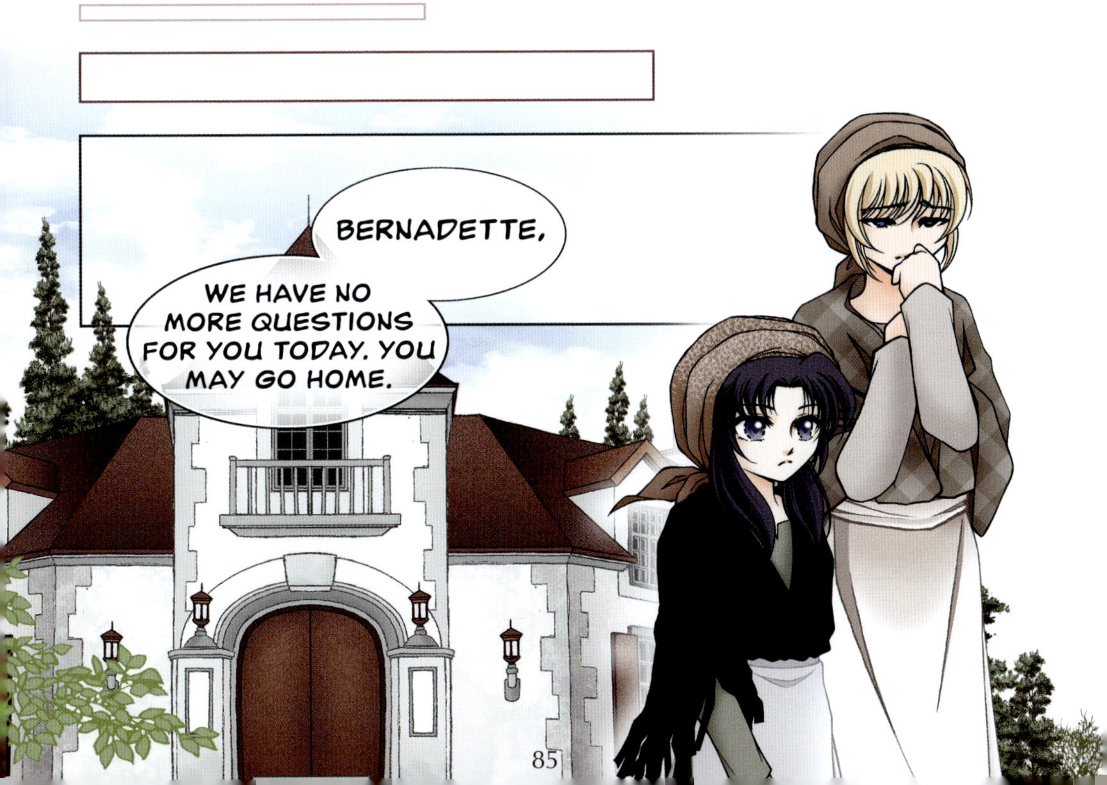

BERNADETTE,

WE HAVE NO MORE QUESTIONS FOR YOU TODAY. YOU MAY GO HOME.

HOW LONG WILL THEY KEEP INTERROGATING YOU WITH THE SAME QUESTIONS OVER AND OVER?

MARCH 25, 1858
BERNADETTE!
WHERE ARE YOU GOING IN MIDDLE OF THE NIGHT?
벌떡!
SPRING!
다다다닥
DASH

다다다—
THUMP
다다다—
THUMP
다다다—
THUMP
PLEASE TELL ME YOUR NAME.
I BEG YOU.

"I AM THE
IMMACULATE CONCEPTION."*

*THIS MEANS THAT MARY WAS CONCEIVED WITHOUT ORIGINAL SIN.

KNOCK
KNOCK
KNOCK
쾅 쾅 쾅
WHO IS IT? IT'S SO EARLY IN THE MORNING . . .
HUH? BERNADETTE, WHAT IS IT?
I FOUND OUT!
WHAT?
HER NAME!
WHOSE?
THE IMMACULATE CONCEPTION!
HUH?
비몽
SLEEPY . . .
사몽
OH, IS THAT SO? THE LADY'S NAME IS . . .

*WHEN MARY WAS TOLD SHE WOULD CONCEIVE JESUS.

SO I KEPT ON REPEATING THEM AS I RAN HERE TO YOU.
AND SHE ASKED FOR A CHAPEL . . .
하아
SIGH
BERNADETTE, GO BACK HOME FOR NOW.
I WILL CALL YOU HERE LATER.
THE ASSISTANT PASTOR, FATHER POMIAN.

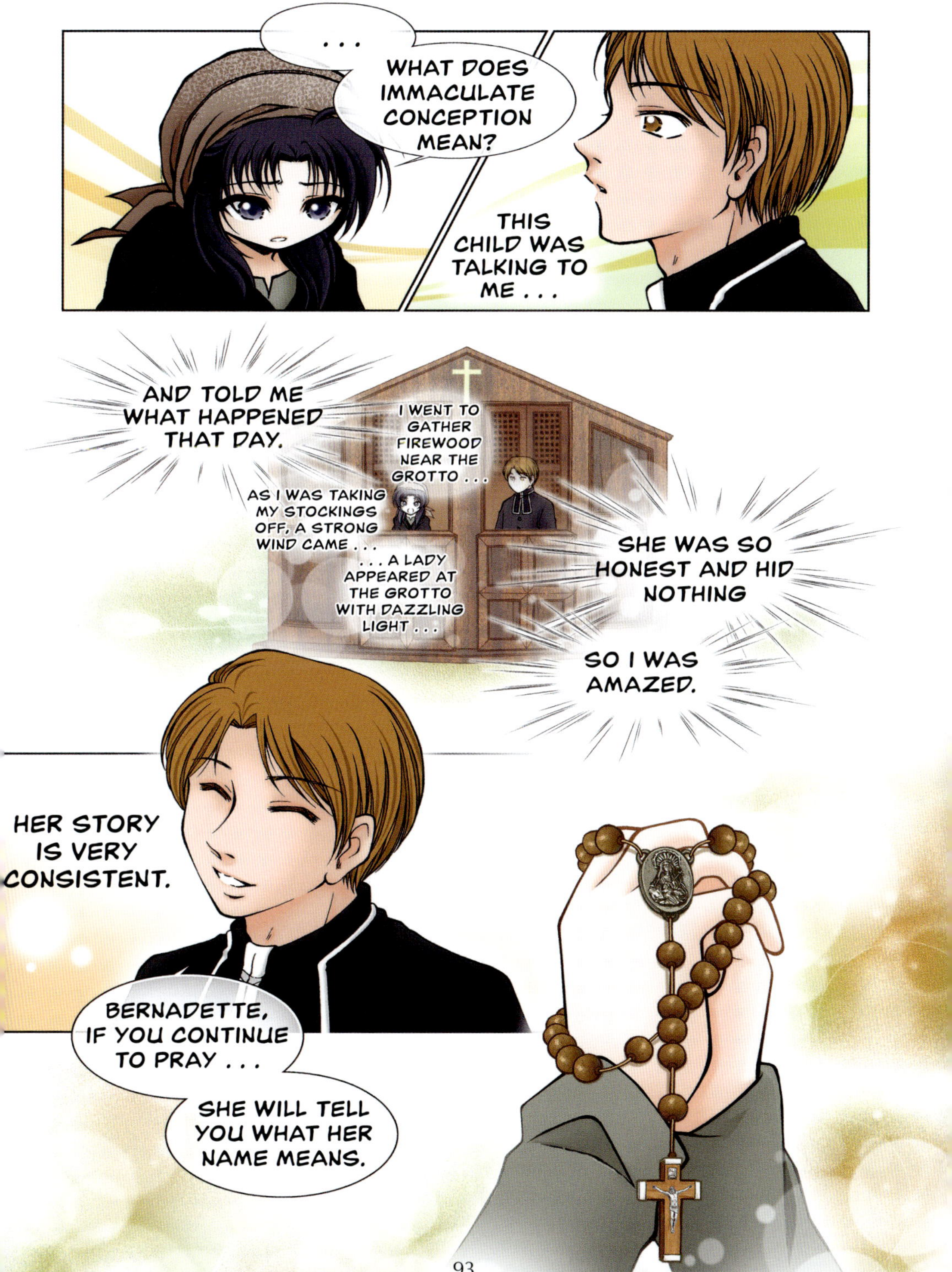

AND TOLD ME WHAT HAPPENED THAT DAY.

I WENT TO GATHER FIREWOOD NEAR THE GROTTO . . .

AS I WAS TAKING MY STOCKINGS OFF, A STRONG WIND CAME . . .

. . . A LADY APPEARED AT THE GROTTO WITH DAZZLING LIGHT . . .

SHE WAS SO HONEST AND HID NOTHING

SO I WAS AMAZED.

HER STORY IS VERY CONSISTENT.

BERNADETTE, IF YOU CONTINUE TO PRAY . . .

SHE WILL TELL YOU WHAT HER NAME MEANS.

...
VIRGIN MARY,
WHO WAS CONCEIVED
WITHOUT ORIGINAL SIN,
HEAR MY PRAYER . . .
"VIRGIN MARY WHO WAS
CONCEIVED WITHOUT
ORIGINAL SIN."
OH . . .
THE LADY WAS . . .

THE VIRGIN MARY!!!

THAT LITTLE GIRL
ISN'T TRIPPING UP ON ANY OF MY QUESTIONS.
쾅!
BAM!
HEY, YOU! DID YOU COMPLETE THE ASSIGNMENT I GAVE YOU?
SIR, AS YOU ORDERED, MANY DOCTORS EXAMINED HER.
THE RESULTS SHOWED THAT NOT ONLY IS SHE PHYSICALLY HEALTHY
BUT ALSO MENTALLY HEALTHY . . .
WE HAVE NO EXCUSE TO ARREST BERNADETTE.
AARGH! SO FRUSTRATING!

BUT NOTHING HAPPENED ON THAT LAST DAY . . .
SO NOW MANY PEOPLE ARE TURNING THEIR BACK ON BERNADETTE, SAYING THAT SHE FOOLED THEM.
SHOULDN'T WE JUST LET IT BE?
NO. I DON'T LIKE THIS BUSINESS WITH THE LADY'S SECRETS . . .
WE NEED TO KEEP ON WATCHING.
YES, SIR . . .
SO ANNOYING . . .
PUT UP FENCES AT THE GROTTO SO THAT NO ONE CAN GO NEAR IT!
쾅
HAMMER
쾅
HAMMER
쾅
HAMMER
OFF LIMITS
IT IS ILLEGAL TO PRAY HERE.
-CHIEF OFFICER

CAN YOU BELIEVE WE HAVE TO STAND HERE AND KEEP WATCH ALL DAY?
I KNOW . . .
I KEPT THE PROMISE OF COMING HERE FOR FIFTEEN DAYS.
GOODBYE, VIRGIN MARY . . .

Trial and Approval

SATAN!
IT IS CERTAIN THAT THE CHILD SAW SATAN.
BECAUSE SATAN HAS HOOFED FEET LIKE AN ANIMAL,
IT MUST HAVE BEEN USING THE ROSES TO HIDE THEM.
THE MIRACLES OF THE SPRING WATER AND THE SO-CALLED THREE SECRETS TOLD BY MARY ARE ALL LIES.
BROTHERS AND SISTERS, DO NOT BE FOOLED BY SATAN'S TRICKS!
DEAR SAINT!

SAINT BERNADETTE!
OUR LITTLE SAINT,
PLEASE BLESS US.
ARE YOU CRAZY?
IF YOU WANT A BLESSING, ASK THE PRIEST!
DEAR SAINT, PLEASE BLESS ME . . .
STOP THAT! A BLESSING IS SOMETHING THAT THE PRIEST GIVES ME!
PLEASE LEAVE ME ALONE!

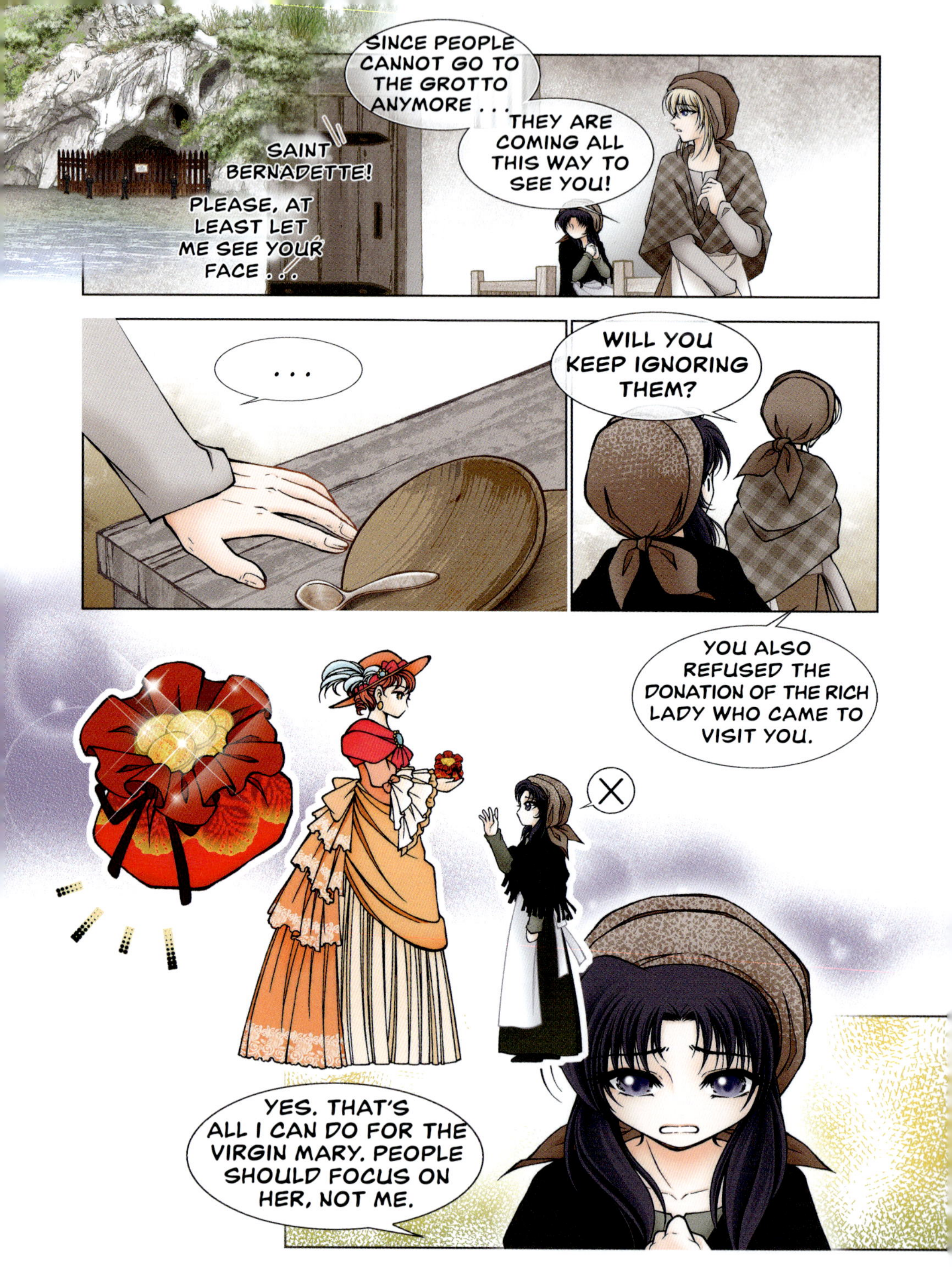

. . .

WILL YOU KEEP IGNORING THEM?

YOU ALSO REFUSED THE DONATION OF THE RICH LADY WHO CAME TO VISIT YOU.

YES. THAT'S ALL I CAN DO FOR THE VIRGIN MARY. PEOPLE SHOULD FOCUS ON HER, NOT ME.

BERNADETTE, PLEASE GIVE ME A BLESSING . . .
꿍
PUSH
DEAR SAINT . . .
WHAT'S MAKING YOU SO HAPPY?
SLAM!
탁!
OH, SISTER!
SOMEONE ASKED ME TO BRING THEM SOME SPRING WATER, SO I DID. THEY GAVE ME THIS IN RETURN FOR DOING THEM A FAVOR.
IT'S A GOLD COIN! GOLD!
흠칫!
GASP!

쨍그랑—!
CLINK!
YOU SOLD THE SPRING WATER FOR MONEY?! ARE YOU INSANE? IT'S A FREE GIFT FROM GOD, WE HAVE NO RIGHT TO SELL IT!
WAAAH . . .
FIND THAT PERSON AND RETURN THIS COIN RIGHT AWAY!
GO ON, GO!

I CAN'T LIVE LIKE THIS!
THE WAY THAT PEOPLE LOOK UP TO ME INSTEAD OF TO THE VIRGIN MARY . . .
IT ISN'T RIGHT!
꽈악!
CLENCH
I DON'T WANT TO BE SEPARATED FROM MY FAMILY, BUT . . .
I MUST LEAVE HOME.
NURSING HOME OF LOURDES
BERNADETTE WENT TO THE NURSING HOME RUN BY THE SISTERS OF CHARITY OF NEVERS, WHERE SHE WAS ABLE TO ATTEND SCHOOL.

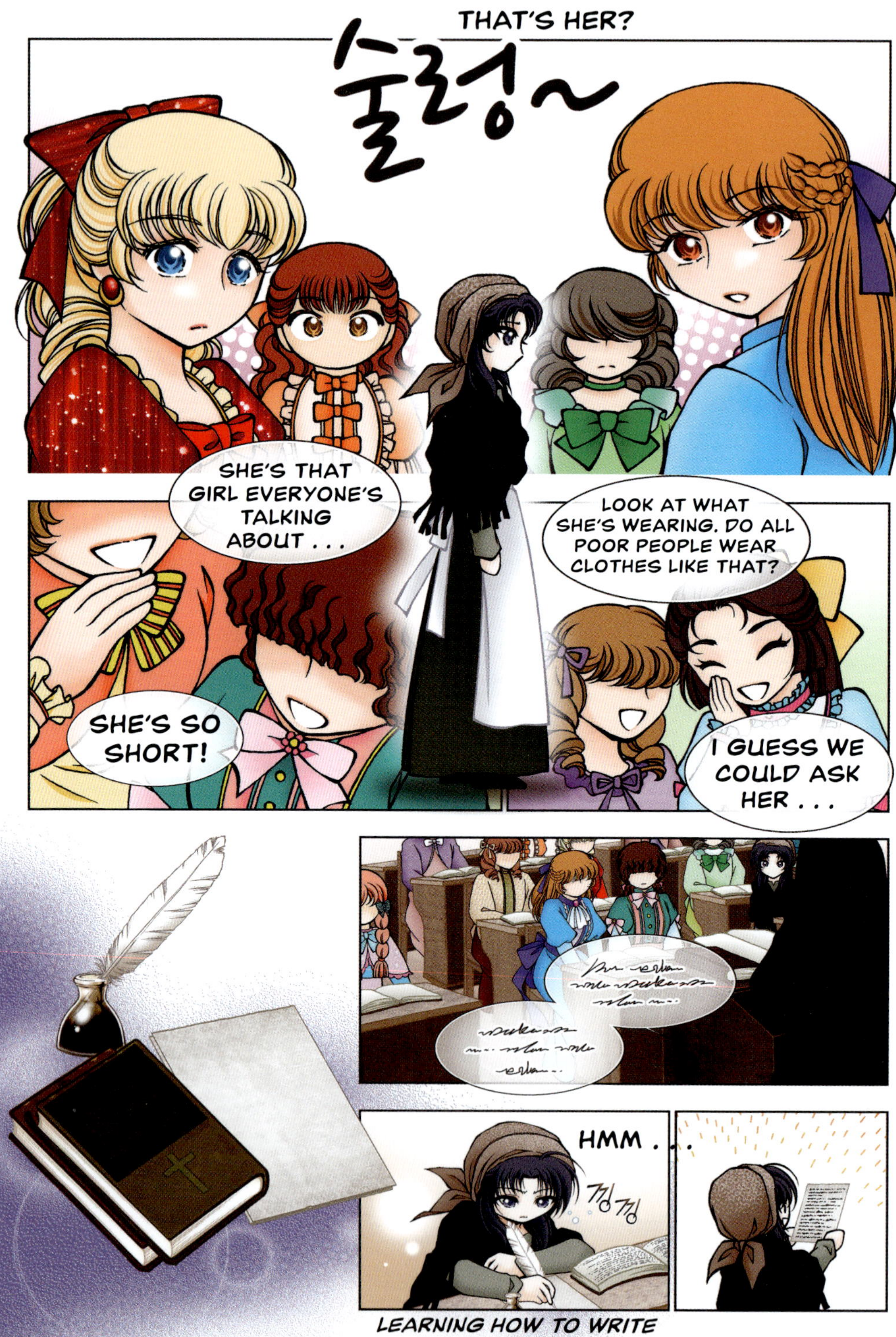

LEARNING HOW TO WRITE

I DON'T KNOW IF IT'S BECAUSE SHE'S SO SHORT, BUT
EEEE!
꺄~아♥
YAY!
꺅꺅
꺅
BERNADETTE OFTEN SPENDS TIME WITH THE YOUNGER GIRLS.
BERNADETTE, SINCE YOU'RE TOO WEAK TO JUMP YOU CAN SWING THE ROPE FOR US.
WOW, IT'S SO PRETTY!

DON'T YOU THINK SO?
I LOVE THIS NEW CORSET.* AND THE CRINOLINE* IS A NEW DESIGN TOO!
IT'S LIGHTER AND ADDS VOLUME TO THE DRESS.
*CORSET: AN UNDERGARMENT WORN TO TRAIN THE TORSO INTO A DESIRED SHAPE.
*CRINOLINE: A STIFF, BELL-SHAPED PETTICOAT WORN UNDER A DRESS.
I'M GOING TO ASK MY MOM TO BUY THEM FOR ME TOO.
I ALSO GOT THIS LUXURY MAKEUP POWDER . . .
OH! THIS IS GORGEOUS!
CORSET? CRINOLINE??

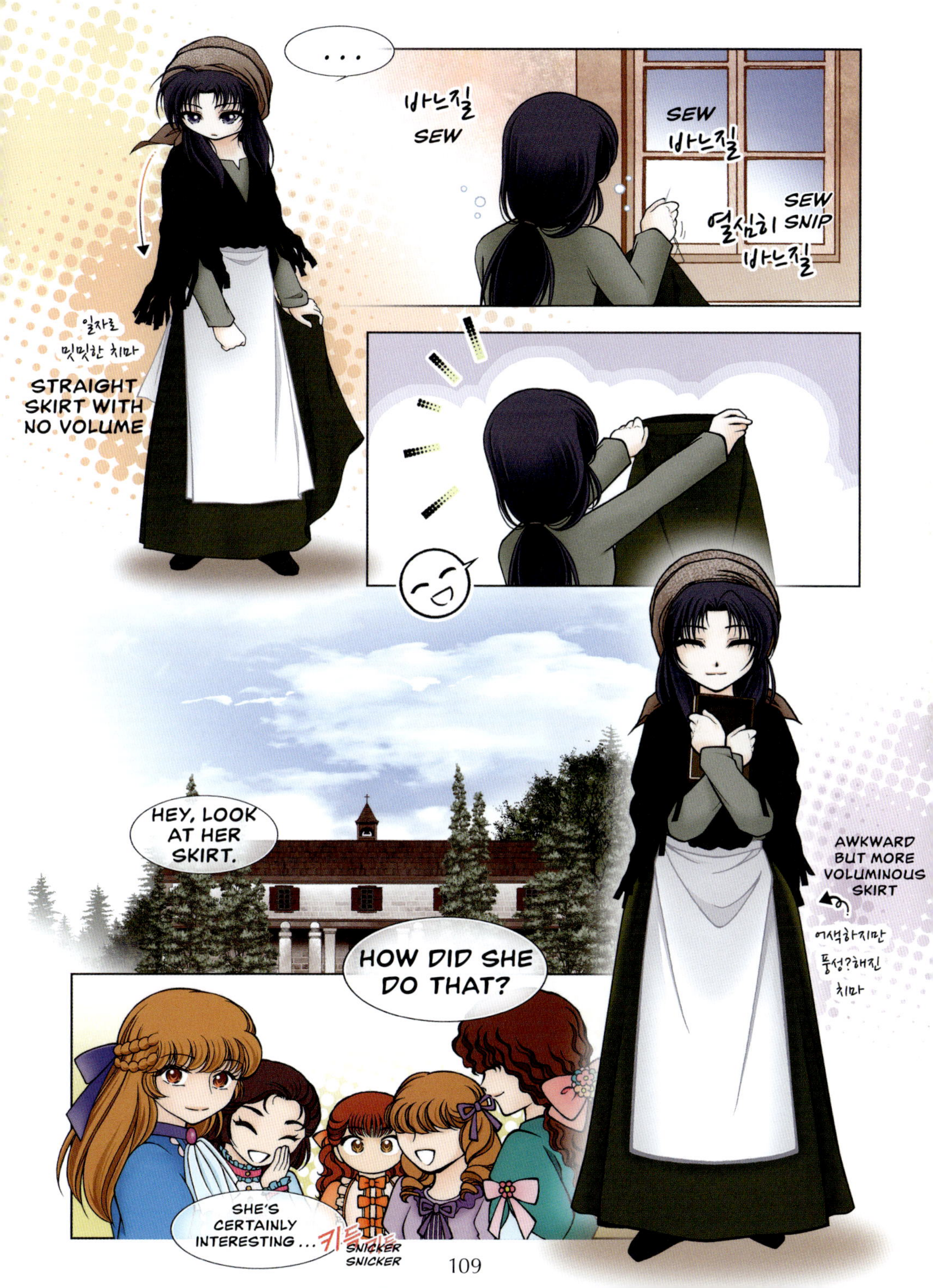
. . .
바느질
SEW
SEW
바느질
SEW
열심히 SNIP
바느질
일자로
밋밋한 치마
STRAIGHT SKIRT WITH NO VOLUME
HEY, LOOK AT HER SKIRT.
HOW DID SHE DO THAT?
AWKWARD BUT MORE VOLUMINOUS SKIRT
어색하지만
풍성?해진
치마
SHE'S CERTAINLY INTERESTING ...
키득키득
SNICKER SNICKER

BERNADETTE!
THIS NOVEL IS REALLY POPULAR RIGHT NOW. YOU SHOULD READ IT TOO.
IT'S FUN! THE MAIN CHARACTER
GETS INTO A HUGE SCANDAL AND . . . BLAH BLAH BLAH . . .
LOVE
오글오글
로맨스
EXOTIC ROMANCE
IF I WERE GOING TO READ THAT KIND OF BOOK,
I WOULD RATHER NOT HAVE LEARNED HOW TO READ AT ALL.

HMPH. I THOUGHT SHE WANTED TO HANG OUT WITH US.
SHE WAS WATCHING US SO CAREFULLY BEFORE THAT I ASSUMED SHE LIKED THIS KIND OF THING. I GUESS NOT.
부욱!
RIP!
팡 팡
PAT PAT
BACK TO NORMAL

. . .
I . . .
IN ORDER TO BUILD A CHURCH, WE NEED DONATIONS.
AH!
PLEASE PUT IT IN THE DONATION BOX . . .
TO BUILD MARY'S CHURCH.

DECEMBER 7, 1860
THE LAST OFFICIAL INVESTIGATION
BERNADETTE,
I WILL BEGIN THE INVESTIGATION.

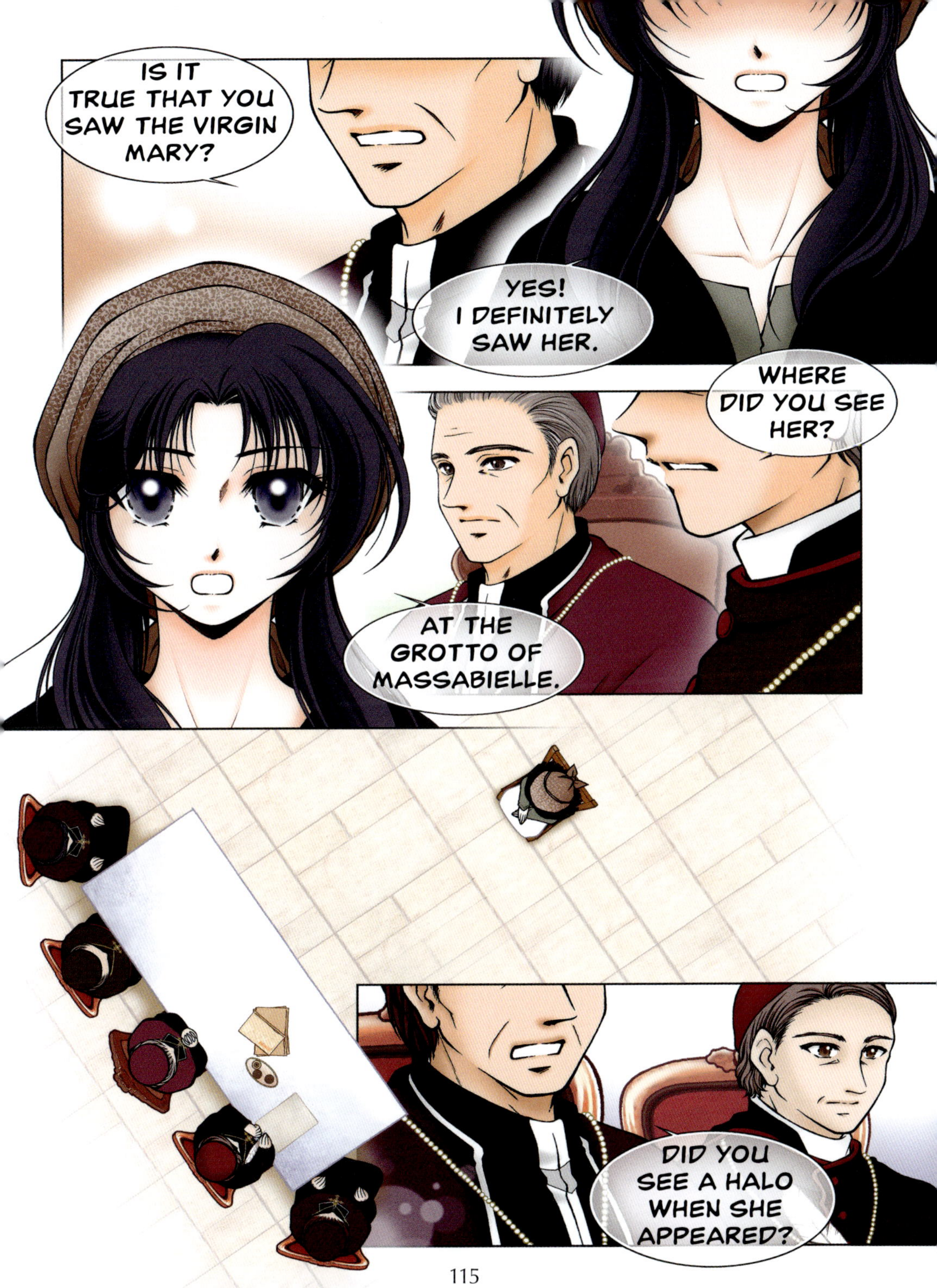
IS IT TRUE THAT YOU SAW THE VIRGIN MARY?
YES! I DEFINITELY SAW HER.
WHERE DID YOU SEE HER?
AT THE GROTTO OF MASSABIELLE.
DID YOU SEE A HALO WHEN SHE APPEARED?

. . .
THE VIRGIN MARY WAS SURROUNDED BY A DAZZLING LIGHT.
DID YOU SEE THE LIGHT AND THE VIRGIN MARY AT THE SAME TIME?
NO. I SAW THE LIGHT BEFORE THE VIRGIN MARY APPEARED,
AND IT LASTED A LITTLE WHILE EVEN AFTER SHE DISAPPEARED.
IF IT IS TRUE THAT YOU HEARD THREE SECRETS FROM THE VIRGIN MARY
TELL US WHAT THEY ARE.
I CANNOT TELL YOU. I PROMISED I WOULD NOT TELL ANYONE.*
*BERNADETTE REMAINED FAITHFUL TO HER PROMISE AND NEVER SHARED THE SECRETS ENTRUSTED TO HER BY THE VIRGIN MARY.

I HEARD YOU ATE GRASS AT THE GROTTO.
IT'S HARD TO UNDERSTAND WHY THE VIRGIN MARY WOULD ASK YOU TO DO THAT.
WHY DID YOU DO SUCH A THING?
BECAUSE THE VIRGIN MARY ASKED ME TO.
BERNADETTE,

WHEN THE VIRGIN MARY TOLD YOU THAT SHE IS THE "IMMACULATE CONCEPTION,"
CAN YOU DEMONSTRATE TO ME HOW SHE SAID IT?
덜컹
SCRAPE
벌떡!
RISE
스ㅡ
LIFT

"I AM THE
IMMACULATE
CONCEPTION."

BISHOP LAURENCE . . .

쓰스슥—
SCRITCH SCRATCH

BASED ON THE FACTS AS INDICATED ABOVE, THE CHURCH ACCEPTS AS A TRUTH THAT THE VIRGIN MARY, WHO IS THE IMMACULATE CONCEPTION, HAS APPEARED TO BERNADETTE.
JANUARY 18, 1862

Decision and Farewell

THUMP THUMP THUMP
다다다다다-···
I'LL CHANGE YOUR BED SHEET.
HOW ARE YOU FEELING?
BERNADETTE, WE NEED MORE SHEETS. PLEASE HURRY.
YES, I'M BRINGING MORE.

DID YOU SEE THE NEW PATIENT WHO CAME IN? IT'S HORRIBLE!
SHE FELL INTO A FIRE WHILE SHE WAS DRUNK. SHE'S SEVERELY BURNT . . .
I SHOULDN'T BE TELLING YOU THIS, BUT . . .
YES, IT'S NOT EASY TO HANDLE THAT KIND OF PATIENT . . .
IT HURTS . . . OW!
WRING! 꽈악!
주루룩
DRIP DRIP

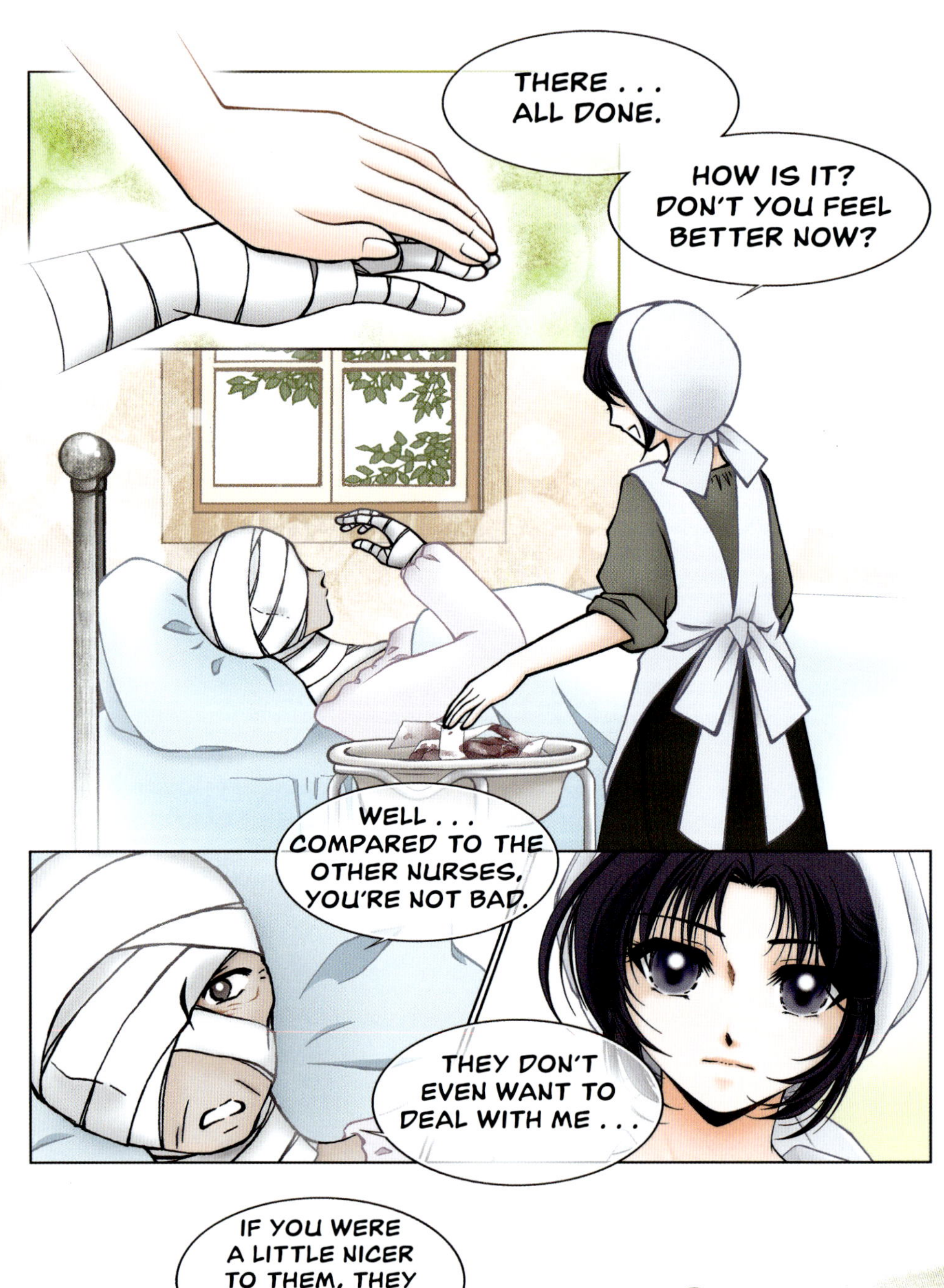
THERE . . .
ALL DONE.
HOW IS IT? DON'T YOU FEEL BETTER NOW?
WELL . . . COMPARED TO THE OTHER NURSES, YOU'RE NOT BAD.
THEY DON'T EVEN WANT TO DEAL WITH ME . . .
IF YOU WERE A LITTLE NICER TO THEM, THEY WOULDN'T ACT THAT WAY.
HMPH! I DON'T NEED THEM!

절뚝
LIMP

GOING HOME?
CONGRATULATIONS!
DON'T GET DRUNK ANYMORE SO YOU WON'T HAVE TO COME BACK HERE.

HA! I'LL QUIT DRINKING SO I WON'T HAVE TO SEE YOU AGAIN.

GOOD RIDDANCE!

절뚝
LIMP

LIMP LIMP
절뚝
절뚝

THANKS FOR WHAT YOU DID . . .

스슥-- 슥--
SWISH SWISH
WHEW. THIS STAIN WON'T COME OFF . . .
UGH, THE SMELL . . .
WASH THIS TOO.
열심 열심히
WORKING HARD
부걱 부걱 부걱
SCRUB SCRUB
AH.
후우
WHEW!
BERNADETTE, AREN'T YOU TIRED?
FATHER POMIAN.

EVERY TIME I SEE YOU, YOU'RE DOING THE HARD WORK NOBODY ELSE WANTS TO DO . . .
I'M OKAY.
I LIKE TAKING CARE OF THE MOST DIFFICULT PEOPLE. IT IS LIKE CARING FOR JESUS HIMSELF.

BERNADETTE, YOU HAVE A GUEST.
OH!

ON SEPTEMBER 27, 1863, THE BISHOP OF NEVERS, BISHOP FORCADE, CAME TO SEE BERNADETTE WHILE HE WAS VISITING LOURDES.
BERNADETTE, WHAT KIND OF WORK DO YOU WANT TO DO FROM NOW ON?
AS LONG AS I CAN KEEP SERVING GOD AND HIS PEOPLE, I'M HAPPY.
I JUST WANT TO CONTINUE LIVING HERE.
WELL . . . THAT MIGHT BE A BIT DIFFICULT.
WHY?
BECAUSE YOU ARE A BOARDING STUDENT,
AND DON'T HAVE A PERMANENT PLACE HERE.

YOU ARE NEITHER A NUN NOR AN EMPLOYEE,
SO YOU WON'T BE ABLE TO STAY HERE FOREVER.
. . .
SINCE YOU ARE NO LONGER A CHILD
IT MAY BE BEST FOR YOU TO STUDY OR FIND A JOB.
BUT I LOVE IT HERE!
벌떡!
RISE!
I DON'T KNOW MUCH ABOUT ANYTHING . . .
AND I CAN'T DO WORK WELL LIKE OTHERS DO.
I WANT TO BECOME A NUN . . .
AND DEDICATE MY WHOLE LIFE TO JESUS, BUT MY FAMILY IS SO POOR . . .

BERNADETTE, YOU HAVE TALENT.
I SAW YOU WORKING VERY WELL JUST A MOMENT AGO.
REALLY? WHAT TALENT?
PEELING CARROTS!
YOU WERE PEELING THOSE CARROTS PERFECTLY.
. . .
PFFT!
푸훗!
HA HA HA . . . THAT'S NOT A REAL TALENT.
YOUR EXCELLENCY, YOU MAKE JOKES TOO?
GOD LOVES EVEN CARROT-PEELERS.
IF YOUR HEART IS IN YOUR WORK, THAT IS ENOUGH.

IF GOD IS CALLING YOU TO BE A NUN, THEN YOU DON'T NEED TO WORRY. THINGS WILL WORK OUT.
TAKE TIME AND PRAY ABOUT IT.

APRIL 4, 1864
PROCESSION TO DEDICATE THE
STATUE OF THE VIRGIN MARY
(DUE TO ASTHMA, BERNADETTE
WAS UNABLE TO ATTEND)

MOTHER SUPERIOR.
BERNADETTE, WHAT IS IT?
I BELIEVE GOD IS CALLING ME TO BECOME A NUN.
AND I THINK I KNOW THE CONVENT I WOULD LIKE TO ENTER.
YOU DID? WHERE IS IT?
IT'S YOUR CONVENT, THE SISTERS OF CHARITY OF NEVERS.

COUGH
쿨럭 쿨럭
COUGH COUGH
쿨럭
꽈악!
CLENCH
IS SHE OKAY NOW?
SHE WAS VERY ILL JUST A FEW DAYS AGO, ALMOST ON THE POINT OF DEATH . . .
. . . ENTRANCE INTO THE CONVENT HAS BEEN DELAYED . . .
BECAUSE BERNADETTE IS NOT WELL,
DON'T BOTHER HER WITH MANY QUESTIONS OR REQUESTS.
웅성 웅성
CHATTER CHATTER
와글
MURMUR

BERNADETTE
ON MAY 19, THE CRYPT SANCTUARY AT THE GROTTO WILL BE CONSECRATED. PLEASE BE PRESENT.
EEEEE!
꺄~아♥
우글 우글
CHATTER CHATTER
MAY 19, 1866 –THE CRYPT SANCTUARY CONSECRATION CEREMONY
SO MANY OF THESE CURIOUS PEOPLE ARE SEARCHING FOR ENTERTAINMENT, NOT GOD
. . . I HOPE I CAN ENTER THE CONVENT SOON.
OKAY, I'M GOING TO TAKE SOME PICTURES NOW. LOOK THIS WAY,
HOLD STILL AND DON'T MOVE.

CLICK!
찰칵!
찰칵!
CLICK!
찰칵!
CLICK!
찰칵!
CLICK!
찰칵!
CLICK!

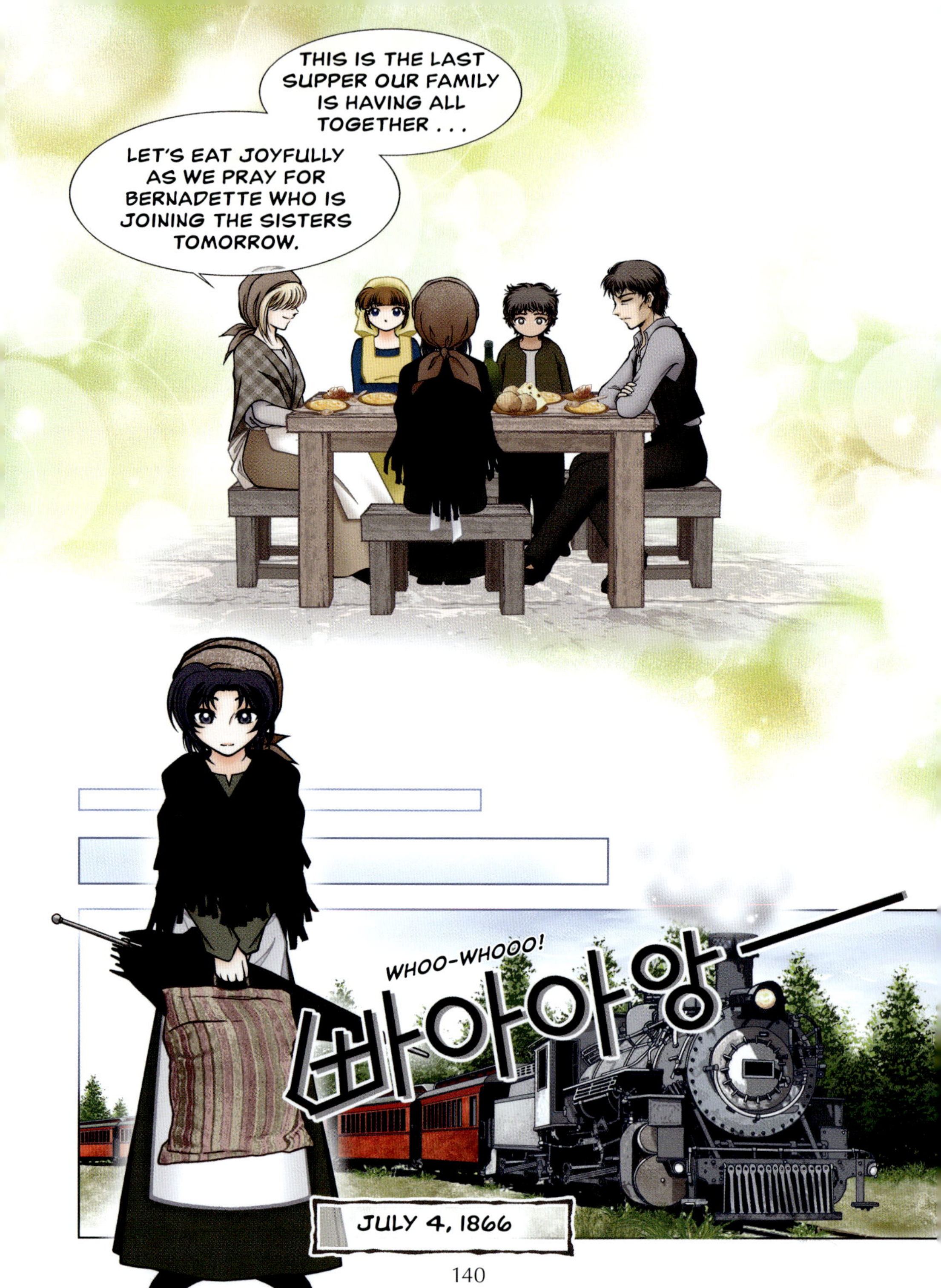

WHOO-WHOOO!

빠아아앙

JULY 4, 1866

GOODBYE,
MASSABIELLE.

GOODBYE,
LOURDES.

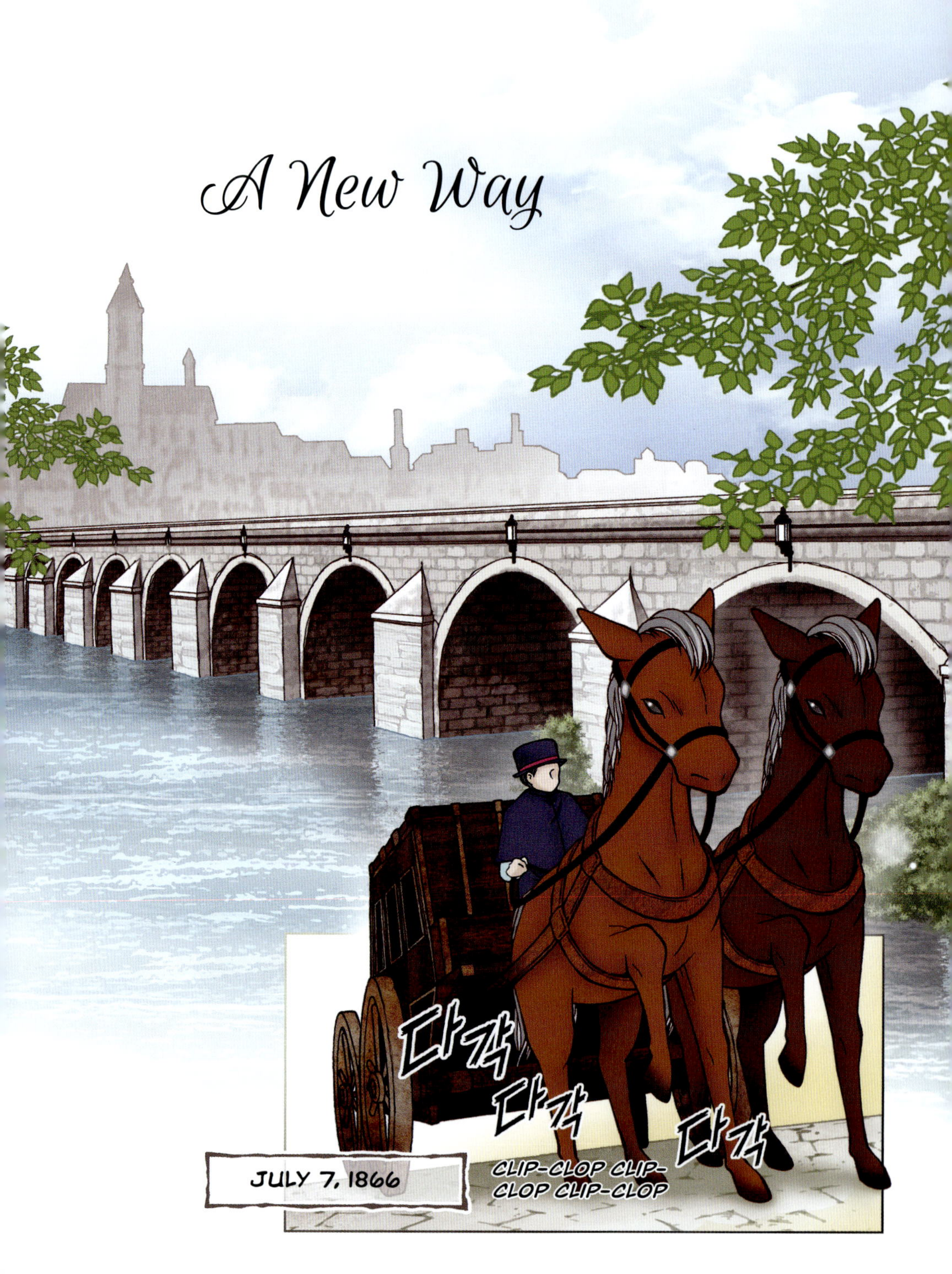
A New Way
다각
다각
다각
CLIP-CLOP CLIP-CLOP CLIP-CLOP
JULY 7, 1866

SCREECH...
덜컹
RATTLE RATTLE
끼익—
MOTHERHOUSE OF THE SISTERS OF CHARITY OF NEVERS
WELCOME TO OUR NEWEST SISTERS.

YOU'VE HAD A LONG TRIP, SO GET A GOOD NIGHT'S REST.
STARTING TOMORROW YOU WILL HAVE MANY THINGS TO LEARN.
. . . SO THAT DAY
I LOOKED UP AT THE GROTTO AND SAW THE VIRGIN MARY.
SHE WAS BEAUTIFUL . . .
I WENT TO THE GROTTO FOR FIFTEEN DAYS AS I HAD PROMISED . . .
AND WHEN I FOLLOWED THE VIRGIN MARY'S INSTRUCTIONS,
I FOUND A SMALL SPRING THERE.
AND THE VIRGIN MARY . . .

BERNADETTE, WELL DONE.
OH, YOU CAME FROM LOURDES WITH ME ON THE TRAIN . . .
I'M LÉONTINE. I AM SO HAPPY TO BE LIVING WITH YOU.
LET'S DO OUR BEST.
YES, LET'S.
JULY 19, 1866
YOU ARE NOW STARTING YOUR TRAINING AS NOVICES.
DURING THIS PERIOD, YOU WILL BE LIVING WITH THE SISTERS AND DOING EVERYTHING THEY DO. WE WILL FOCUS ON PRAYER . . .

BERNADETTE, MAY CHRIST BE WITH YOU AND TEACH YOU
TO LIVE IN GOD'S DIVINE TRUTH AND LOVE.

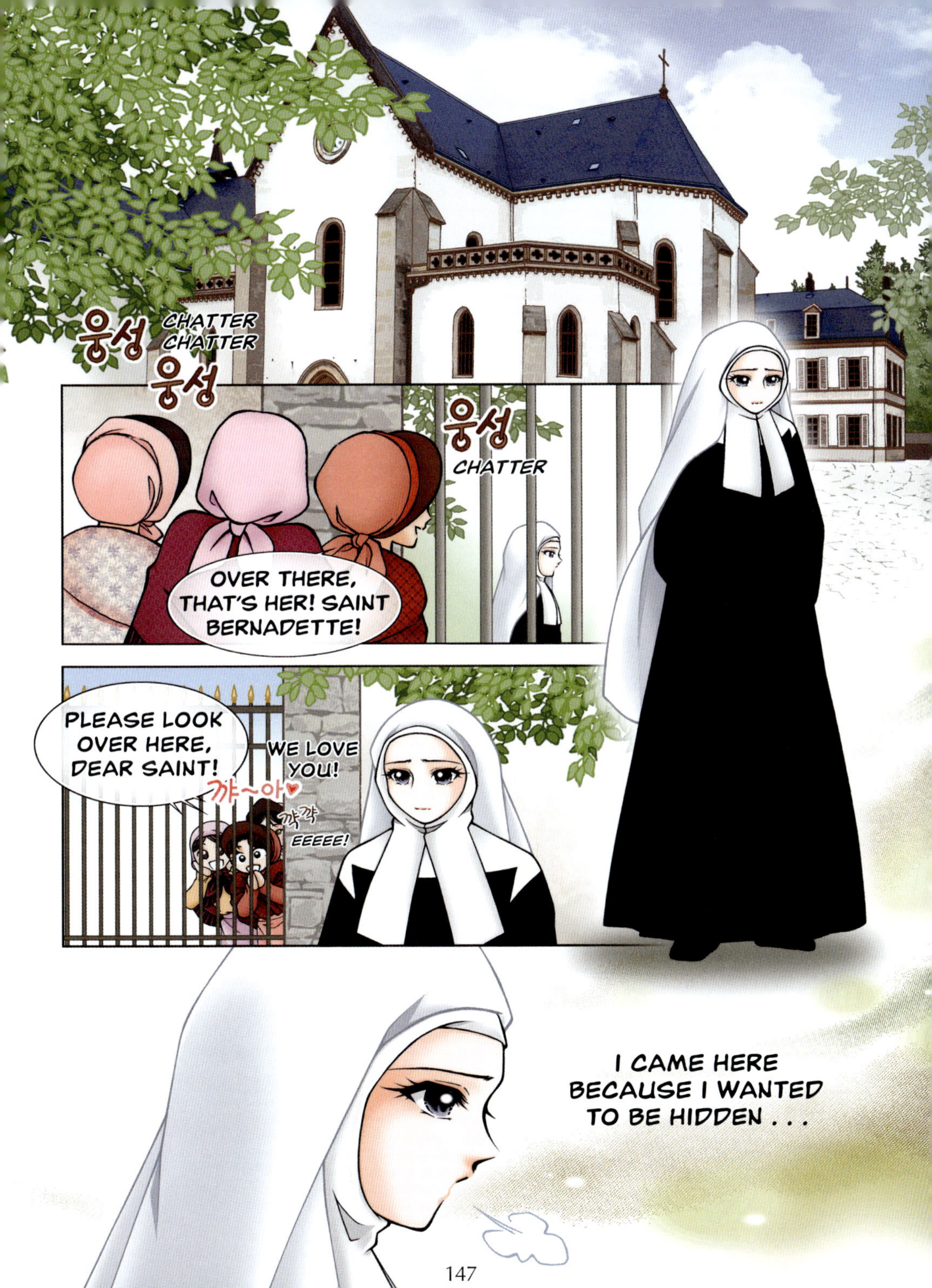

웅성
CHATTER CHATTER
웅성
웅성
CHATTER
OVER THERE, THAT'S HER! SAINT BERNADETTE!
PLEASE LOOK OVER HERE, DEAR SAINT!
WE LOVE YOU!
꺄~아
꺅꺅
EEEEE!
I CAME HERE BECAUSE I WANTED TO BE HIDDEN . . .

JESUS, IF THIS IS A CROSS I MUST CARRY, I WILL ACCEPT IT GLADLY FOR LOVE OF YOU.
HONESTLY, I WONDER IF THE DECISION TO ACCEPT BERNADETTE INTO OUR MONASTERY WAS THE RIGHT ONE.
SINCE SHE CAME, WE HAVEN'T HAD A DAY OF PEACE AND QUIET.
OF COURSE, THE BISHOP REQUESTED THAT WE ADMIT HER . . .
BUT HAVE YOU SEEN BERNADETTE'S EYES, SISTER?
I BELIEVE LOOKING AT THOSE EYES THAT SAW THE VIRGIN MARY IS ENOUGH. WE MADE THE RIGHT DECISION.
SO PLEASE, DON'T TREAT HER ANY DIFFERENTLY THAN THE OTHER NOVICES.

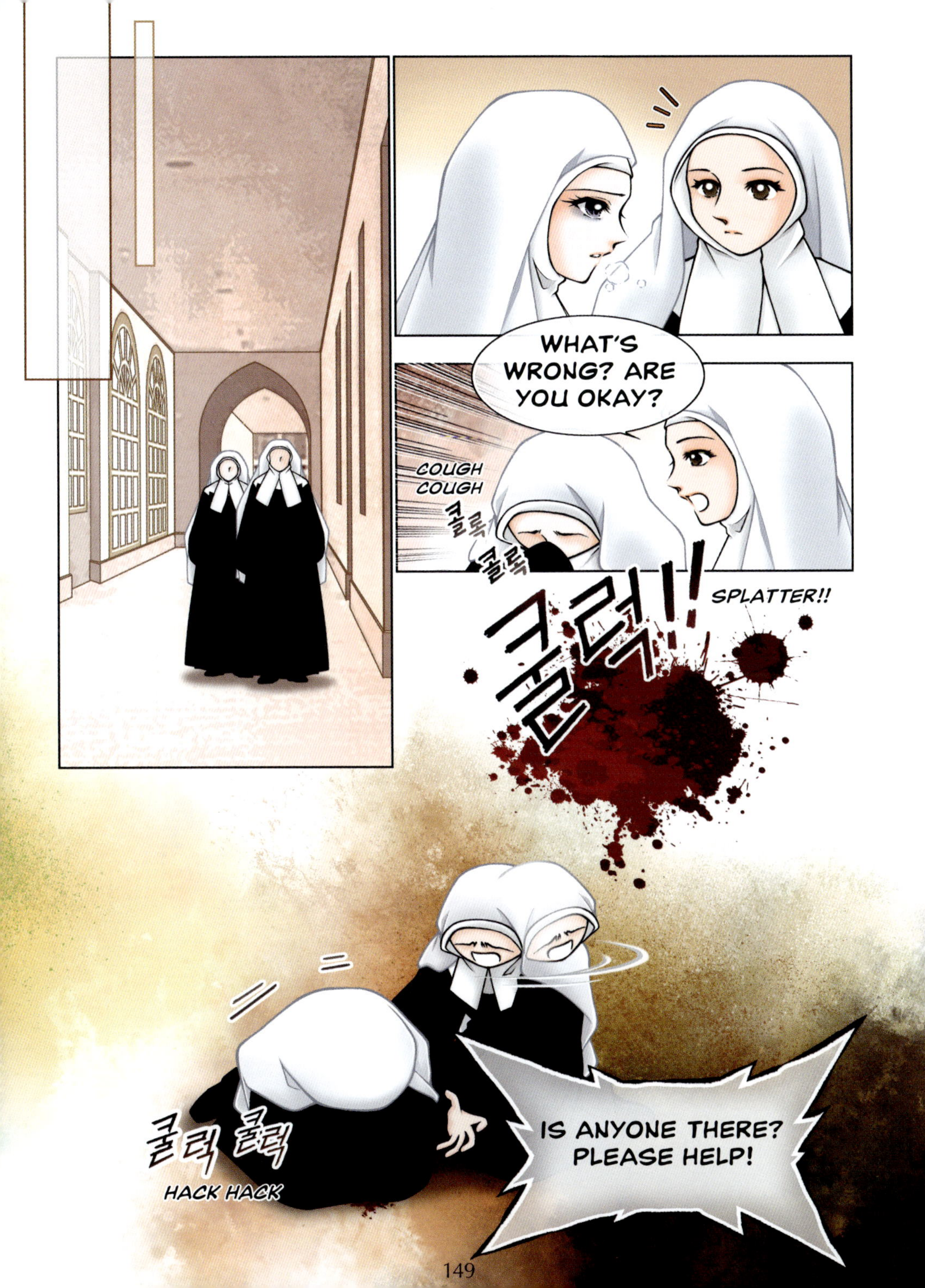
WHAT'S WRONG? ARE YOU OKAY?
COUGH COUGH
콜록
콜록
쿨럭!!
SPLATTER!!
쿨럭 쿨럭
HACK HACK
IS ANYONE THERE? PLEASE HELP!

I THINK BERNADETTE IS CLOSE TO DEATH.
PLEASE PREPARE TO MAKE YOUR VOWS.*
OCTOBER 25, 1866
*VOWS: PROMISES FREELY MADE TO GOD TO DEDICATE ONE'S WHOLE LIFE TO HIM.
I WILL READ THE VOWS FOR YOU.
ANSWER "AMEN" AT THE END.
. . .
. . .
. . .
. . . AMEN.

BOING!
벌떡!
EVEN THOUGH I MADE MY VOWS, I GUESS IT'S NOT GOD'S WILL FOR ME TO DIE TODAY.
I CALLED THE BISHOP BECAUSE I THOUGHT YOU WERE CLOSE TO DEATH . . .
TODAY'S VOWS DON'T COUNT!
BERNADETTE, IF YOU ARE NO LONGER FEELING ILL, YOU WILL CONTINUE YOUR TRAINING TOMORROW.
GLADLY.

MURMUR
MURMUR
DID YOU HEAR? THE VEIL AND THE CROSS SHE RECEIVED DURING THAT CHAOTIC VOW INCIDENT . . .
EVEN THOUGH THE VOWS WERE VOIDED, SHE NEVER RETURNED THEM TO MOTHER SUPERIOR!
PSST!

THEN IT'S STEALING!

AND THE OTHER DAY, THE SISTER IN CHARGE OF THE KITCHEN WAS SCOLDING HER . . .
WHISPER
HOW COULD YOU USE SO MUCH WATER WITHOUT PERMISSION? PUT IT BACK!

SISTER, HOW CAN I PUT WATER BACK?
THAT'S IMPOSSIBLE.
AND SHE WAS SMILING WHEN SHE REPLIED.
REALLY? HOW COULD SHE SMILE WHILE GETTING SCOLDED?

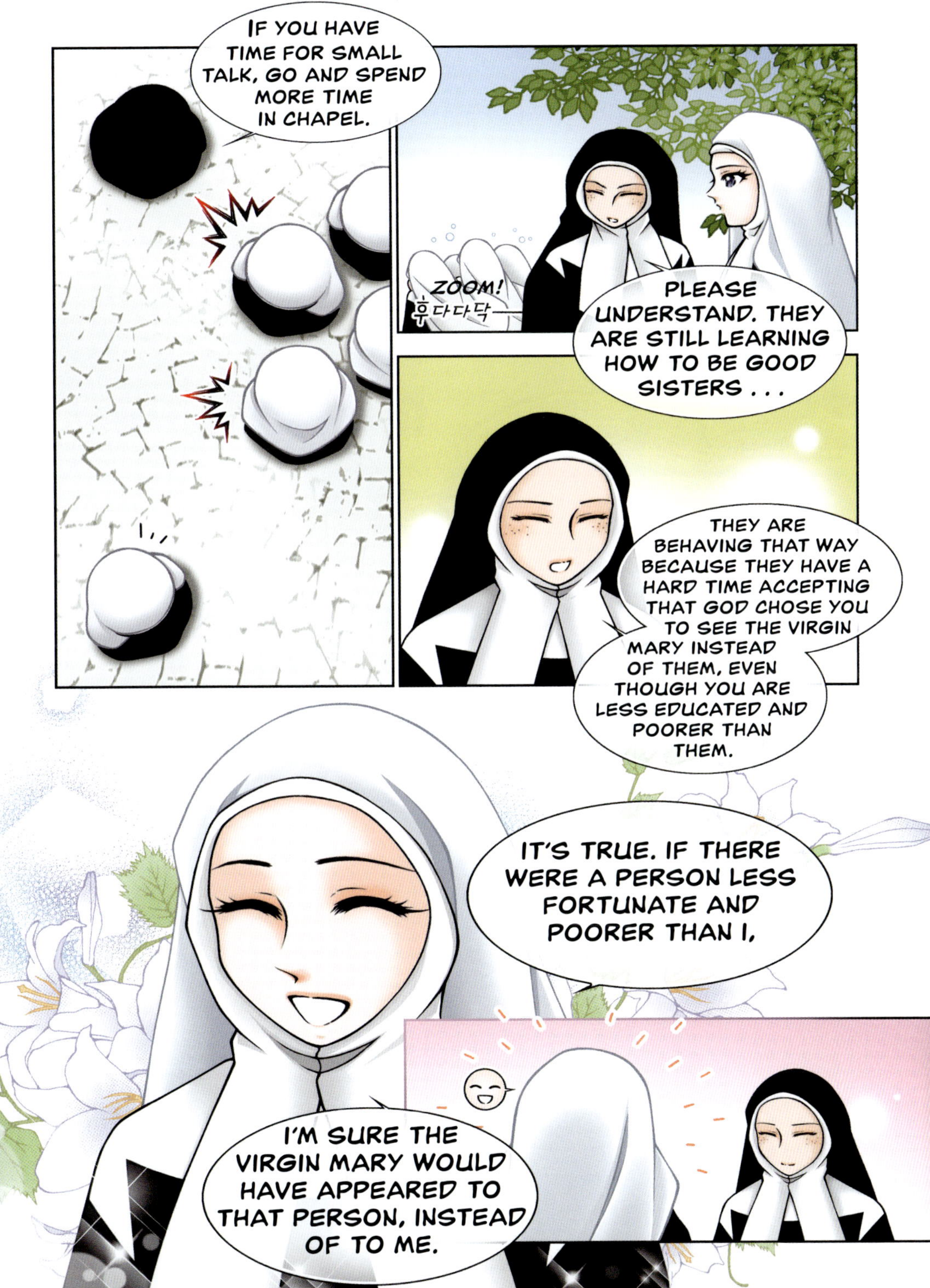
IF YOU HAVE TIME FOR SMALL TALK, GO AND SPEND MORE TIME IN CHAPEL.
ZOOM!
후다다닥
PLEASE UNDERSTAND. THEY ARE STILL LEARNING HOW TO BE GOOD SISTERS . . .
THEY ARE BEHAVING THAT WAY BECAUSE THEY HAVE A HARD TIME ACCEPTING THAT GOD CHOSE YOU TO SEE THE VIRGIN MARY INSTEAD OF THEM, EVEN THOUGH YOU ARE LESS EDUCATED AND POORER THAN THEM.
IT'S TRUE. IF THERE WERE A PERSON LESS FORTUNATE AND POORER THAN I,
I'M SURE THE VIRGIN MARY WOULD HAVE APPEARED TO THAT PERSON, INSTEAD OF TO ME.

OCTOBER 30, 1867
NOW I WILL ANNOUNCE THE ASSIGNMENTS OF THE SISTERS WHO MADE THEIR FIRST VOWS TODAY.
PLEASE PREPARE TO DEPART FOR YOUR NEW ASSIGNMENT AT ONCE.
SISTER MARIA,
YOU ARE ASSIGNED TO THE NURSING HOME AT LOURDES.
SISTER TERESA,
YOU ARE ASSIGNED TO NURSING.
SISTER ANNA, YOU ARE ASSIGNED TO . . .
SISTER SOPHIA, YOU ARE ASSIGNED TO . . .
SISTER VERONICA,
YOU ARE ASSIGNED TO IRELAND.

SISTER BERNADETTE . . .
BISHOP FORCADE,
DUE TO HER FREQUENT ILLNESS, I BELIEVE THAT SISTER BERNADETTE CAN'T HANDLE ANY ASSIGNMENT AT THIS TIME.
I AM PLANNING TO GIVE HER ONLY SMALL TASKS OF PATIENT ROOM CARE AT THE MOTHERHOUSE.
IS THERE REALLY NOTHING THAT SHE CAN DO?
BISHOP, YOU HELPED ME REALIZE IN THE PAST THAT
MY INABILITIES ARE NOT AN OBSTACLE TO GOD WORKING THROUGH ME.
YES, INDEED.
SISTER BERNADETTE, YOUR ASSIGNMENT IS "PRAYER."

. . .
SISTER AGNES!
YOU SHOULD BE IN BED!
SISTER BERNADETTE! I WAS PRAYING . . .
SISTER, YOU ARE A PATIENT. FULFILL YOUR RESPONSIBILITY AS A PATIENT FIRST. YOU NEED REST.
PLEASE, RETURN TO YOUR ROOM!
I WILL DO YOUR SHARE OF PRAYER.
YES . . .

THIS GIRL WILL BE UNDER YOUR CARE STARTING TODAY, SISTER BERNADETTE.
PLEASE GUIDE HER WELL.
SHE'S AT AN AGE WHERE SHE STILL NEEDS HER MOTHER . . .
울먹 울먹
SNIFF SNIFF . . .
스-
COME NOW . . .

THERE . . . YOU MUST MISS YOUR MOM SO MUCH.
THINK OF YOUR MOM
꼬옥
PAT PAT
AND CRY ALL YOU WANT.
으아앙—
WAAAAAH!

1873
COUGH COUGH
쿨럭 쿨럭
COUGH!
쿨럭!!

SISTER BERNADETTE, YOU'RE AWAKE ALREADY?
OH MY! LOOK AT THE SWEAT.
LET ME WIPE YOUR FACE FOR YOU.
THANK YOU.
YOU'VE HAD SUCH A BAD COUGH FROM THE RELAPSE OF TUBERCULOSIS . . .
WHY DIDN'T YOU SAY ANYTHING SOONER?
THIS PLACE . . . THIS PATIENT ROOM IS THE PLACE I WILL SPEND MY TIME FROM NOW ON!

A SMALL
WHITE BED!
LYING IN A
"WHITE CHURCH"
WHILE SHARING
THE PAIN OF
JESUS ON THE
CROSS
IS MY ASSIGNMENT.
I ACCEPT IT WITH
LOVE FOR HIS SAKE.

*PRESSURE ULCER: A PAINFUL INJURY CAUSED BY PROLONGED PRESSURE ON THE SKIN (OFTEN FROM REMAINING IN ONE POSITION FOR TOO LONG).

IT'S NATURAL TO GET PRESSURE ULCERS* FROM LYING DOWN IN BED FOR SO LONG . . .

BUT UNTIL NOW I HADN'T NOTICED THAT SHE HAS THEM . . .

I FOUND ULCERS A MOMENT AGO WHILE I WAS HELPING HER CHANGE HER CLOTHES. THEY WERE SO BAD IT WAS HARD FOR ME TO LOOK AT THEM.

GRIND

드르륵

. . . IS THIS A DREAM?

IS THIS THE MILL WHERE I WAS BORN . . . ? AM I DREAMING . . . ?

YES . . . I AM LIKE THE GRAIN THAT IS BEING GROUND BY THE STONE . . .

UNTIL THE DAY MY LIFE ENDS . . . THIS PAIN WILL CONTINUE . . .

HEY, BERNADETTE!

. . . WHO ARE YOU?

IN THE NAME OF JESUS CHRIST OUR LORD . . .
칫!! AARGH!
슈르륵
POOF!
휴- WHEW . . .
EASTER, 1879
WHAT?! SATAN APPEARED OVERNIGHT AND TORTURED YOU?!

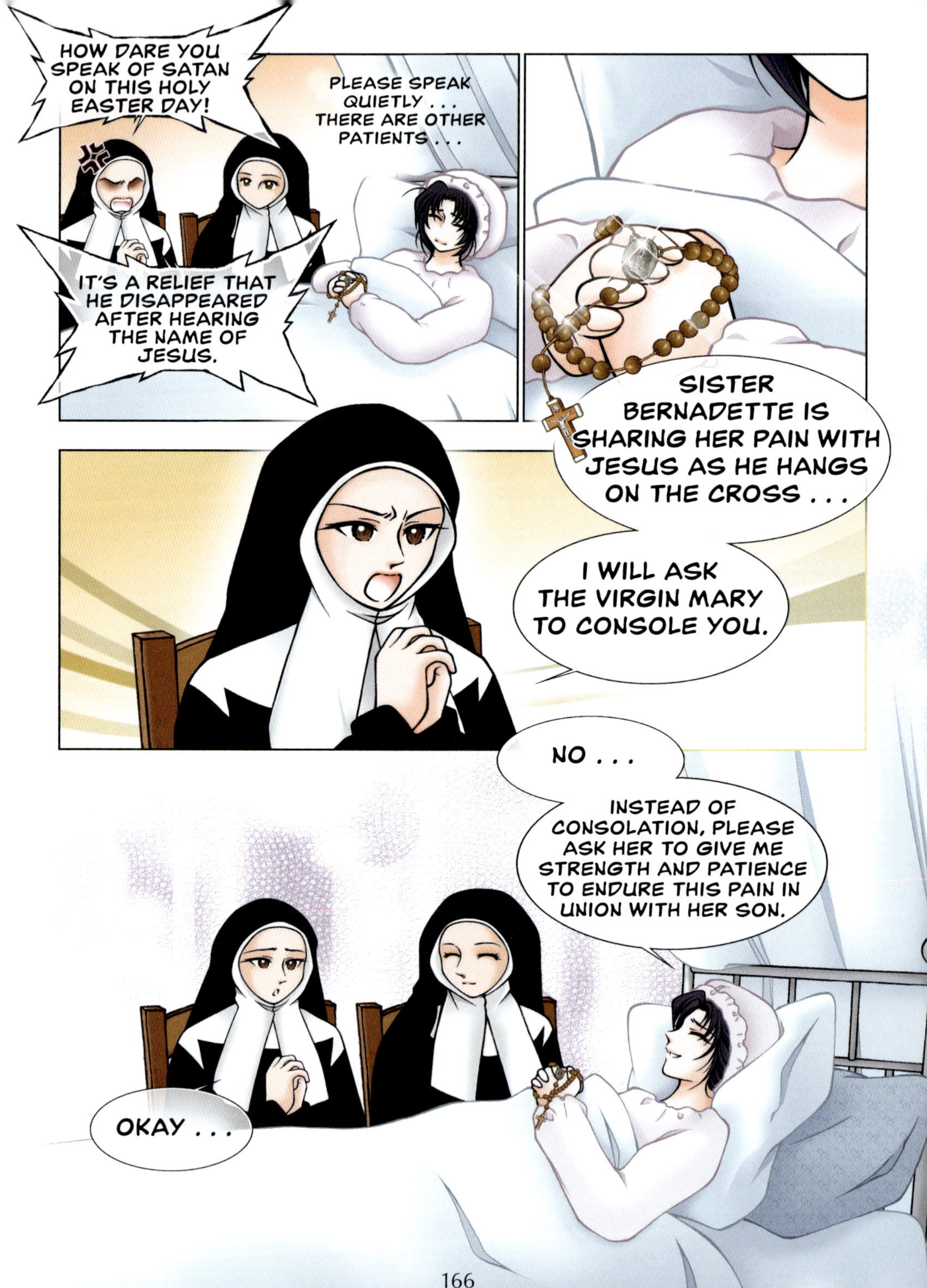
HOW DARE YOU SPEAK OF SATAN ON THIS HOLY EASTER DAY!
IT'S A RELIEF THAT HE DISAPPEARED AFTER HEARING THE NAME OF JESUS.
PLEASE SPEAK QUIETLY . . . THERE ARE OTHER PATIENTS . . .
SISTER BERNADETTE IS SHARING HER PAIN WITH JESUS AS HE HANGS ON THE CROSS . . .
I WILL ASK THE VIRGIN MARY TO CONSOLE YOU.
NO . . .
INSTEAD OF CONSOLATION, PLEASE ASK HER TO GIVE ME STRENGTH AND PATIENCE TO ENDURE THIS PAIN IN UNION WITH HER SON.
OKAY . . .

LORD!
HOLY MARY, MOTHER OF GOD . . .
. . . PRAY FOR US SINNERS . . .
. . .
. . .
. . .

SISTER BERNADETTE, DON'T TRY TO TALK IF IT IS TOO HARD FOR YOU.

I HAVE LIVED WITH DEAF PEOPLE.

I KNOW WHAT YOU WANT JUST BY LOOKING AT YOUR EYES. SO DON'T WORRY.

SISTERS, PLEASE HELP ME.

YES.

BE CAREFUL, NOW.

영차

영차

ONE

TWO

THREE!

영차

GOOD.

WELL DONE, SISTERS.

I THIRST . . .
HOLD ON A MINUTE. I'LL BRING SOME WATER RIGHT AWAY.
THUMP THUMP
후닥후닥ㅡ

HERE, DRINK SLOWLY.
GULP . . .
꿀꺽…

SISTER GABRIELLE.
. . .

WHILE SISTER GABRIELLE AND THREE OTHER SISTERS WERE WITH HER . . .
BERNADETTE PASSED AWAY ON APRIL 16, 1879. HER LAST WORDS WERE, "PRAY FOR ME, A POOR SINNER."

1909

ST. JOSEPH'S CHAPEL
CREAK
끼익—
SO THIS INVESTIGATION FOR BEATIFICATION WILL BE FOR A SISTER WHO WAS ALREADY CALLED A SAINT THIRTY YEARS AGO?
EVEN IF THEY ARE SAINTS, LOOKING AT THEIR DEAD BODIES AFTER SO MANY YEARS IS A LITTLE . . .
저벅 저벅
THUMP THUMP
LET'S STOP THE SMALL TALK AND DO WHAT WE CAME HERE TO DO.
덜컹…
CREEEEAK . . .

털썩
THUD!
A SAINT . . .
SHE REALLY IS A SAINT.

WHEN BERNADETTE'S COFFIN WAS OPENED DURING THE INVESTIGATION FOR HER CAUSE FOR CANONIZATION IN 1909, BERNADETTE'S BODY WAS FOUND JUST THE WAY IT WAS WHEN SHE WAS ALIVE, FREE FROM ANY SIGNS OF DECAY.
HER BODY WAS EXAMINED AGAIN IN 1919 AND 1929, AND IT REMAINED INCORRUPT.
SHE WAS BEATIFIED ON JUNE 14, 1925, AND CANONIZED ON DECEMBER 8, 1933.

"I PROMISE YOU HAPPINESS
NOT IN THIS WORLD
BUT IN HEAVEN."

EDITOR'S NOTE

TODAY, THE GROTTO OF MASSABIELLE WHERE MARY APPEARED TO BERNADETTE RECEIVES MILLIONS OF VISITORS A YEAR. THE SPRING THAT BERNADETTE UNCOVERED IS STILL FLOWING STRONG. PILGRIMS FROM AROUND THE WORLD GATHER AT LOURDES TO PRAY AND TO BE HEALED OF THEIR PHYSICAL AND SPIRITUAL AILMENTS.

Saint Bernadette,
pray for us!

Who are the Daughters of St. Paul?

We are Catholic sisters with a mission. Our task is to bring the love of Jesus to everyone like Saint Paul did. You can find us in over 50 countries. Our founder, Blessed James Alberione, showed us how to reach out to the world through the media. That's why we publish books, make movies and apps, record music, broadcast on radio, perform concerts, help people at our bookstores, visit parishes, use social media and the Internet, and pray for all of you.